Balanchine Variations

Florida A&M University, Tallahassee
Florida Atlantic University, Boca Raton
Florida Gulf Coast University, Ft. Myers
Florida International University, Miami
Florida State University, Tallahassee
New College of Florida, Sarasota
University of Central Florida, Orlando
University of Florida, Gainesville
University of North Florida, Jacksonville
University of South Florida, Tampa
University of West Florida, Pensacola

University Press of Florida

Gainesville · Tallahassee · Tampa

Boca Raton · Pensacola · Orlando · Miami

Jacksonville · Ft. Myers · Sarasota

Balanchine

Variations

Nancy Goldner

Copyright 2008 by Nancy Goldner

BALANCHINE is a Trademark of The George Balanchine Trust.

Printed in the United States of America on acid-free paper

All rights reserved

12 11 10 09   6 5 4 3

Library of Congress Cataloging-in-Publication Data
Goldner, Nancy.
Balanchine variations/Nancy Goldner.
p. cm.
ISBN 978-0-8130-3226-9 (alk. paper)
1. Balanchine, George. 2. Choreographers—United States.
3. Ballet—History. 4. Choreography—History. I. Title.
GV1785.B32G65 2008
792.8'209—dc22   2007038092

The University Press of Florida is the scholarly publishing
agency for the State University System of Florida, comprising
Florida A&M University, Florida Atlantic University, Florida
Gulf Coast University, Florida International University, Florida
State University, New College of Florida, University of Central
Florida, University of Florida, University of North Florida,
University of South Florida, and University of West Florida.

University Press of Florida
15 Northwest 15th Street
Gainesville, FL 32611-2079
www.upf.com

for Jules

Contents

ACKNOWLEDGMENTS   ix

Introduction   1

1928   Apollo   5

1929   Prodigal Son   13

1934   Serenade   19

1941   Concerto Barocco   26

1946   The Night Shadow/La Sonnambula   34

1946   The Four Temperaments   39

1947   Theme and Variations   48

1954   The Nutcracker   53

1954   Western Symphony   59

1957   Square Dance   65

1957   Agon   70

1960   Donizetti Variations   78

1962   A Midsummer Night's Dream   83

1967   Jewels   90

Emeralds   92

Rubies   95

Diamonds   99

1967 Valse Fantaisie 103

1972 The Stravinsky Festival 106

Symphony in Three Movements 108

Stravinsky Violin Concerto 112

Divertimento from Le Baiser de la Fée 117

Duo Concertant 122

1978 Ballo della Regina 126

SUGGESTED READING 131

Acknowledgments

Were it not for Barbara Horgan, Managing Trustee of the George Balan–chine Trust, and Nancy Reynolds, Director of Research of the Balanchine Foundation, this book would not have been written. Horgan gave the lecture series the trust's seal of approval, and Reynolds funded it through the foundation. My gratitude to them runs deep, as it does to Meredith Babb, director of the University Press of Florida, who had the idea of making a book out of my talks about Balanchine. Thank you, too, to the wonderful staff at the University Press of Florida for moving the manuscript along.

My partner in the project, the dancer Merrill Ashley, offered a stimulating perspective from the other side of the footlights. I thank her very much.

Costas, who provided most of the photographs, worked diligently through the process. I am indebted to his good eye, good sense, and good cheer.

The essay on *Agon* first appeared in *Raritan, A Quarterly Review* and the essays on *Prodigal Son* and *The Four Temperaments* first appeared in *Dance Now*. I thank both publications for allowing me to reprint the essays here and am particularly grateful to Allen Robertson, an editor of *Dance Now*, for his encouragement.

For arranging for me to view tapes of many of the Balanchine ballets, I thank Alexandra Felicetti, formerly with the Balanchine Trust and Choreographic Institute. Thank you to Robert Cornfield and David Singer for helping me sort out contractual details. Anna Eberhard Friedlander and Judy Pritchett read the manuscript, and their comments were invaluable.

My father died while I was writing this book, and until his dying day he always remembered to ask how it was going. I am sorry that he did not live to find out.

I owe much of the pleasure of writing this book to my husband, Jules Cohn, whose enthusiasm and critical eye were always in balance.

Introduction

The twenty ballets discussed in this book are drawn from talks I gave across the United States under the auspices of the Balanchine Foundation. They were designed to give the general public an appreciation of whichever Balanchine ballet they were about to see performed by the company that had invited me to speak. Some of these companies are large and located in major cities; others are smaller operations working in small cities; and still others are essentially student groups with big aspirations—hence their inclusion of Balanchine in their repertories.

The table of contents gives a good indication of what the audience outside New York City is able to see of Balanchine's work. It ranges from his earliest surviving piece, *Apollo* (1928), through *Ballo della Regina* (1978). His last ballet premiered in 1981, and he died two years later. There are small-scaled works and a few of the big ones, such as *Jewels* and *A Midsummer Night's Dream*. The really big ones, *Union Jack* and *Vienna Waltzes*, are too large an undertaking, in terms of production as well as number of dancers, for most companies to manage. Only the New York City Ballet performs them, and so they are not included in this book.

Still other large ballets, such as *Symphony in C* and *Stars and Stripes*, are also beyond the means of most United States groups because they require many principal dancers with strong technique. Some groups, of course, can muster the forces to do them justice, but as luck would have it, I never visited a company when it was mounting these ballets. Unfortunately, the great *Liebeslieder Walzer* is hardly ever performed outside the City Ballet, because it requires just the right four couples and decent singers. And still others, such as *Walpurgisnacht Ballet*, simply haven't gone on the circuit yet. There is always another Balanchine ballet to see!

This lecture series began in 1998. In the first years I traveled solo; later I was joined by Merrill Ashley, a former ballerina with the City Ballet, where she now teaches company class and coaches principal dancers. She would discuss the ballets from her perspective as a dancer, and I would talk about what it is like to watch them. What we both liked to concentrate on most was what makes these ballets wonderful.

They were wonderful to me from the start. I began watching Balanchine's ballets in 1949, as a first-grader. The New York City Ballet was a year old, so one could say that the company and I grew up together. At first, I thought his ballets were beautiful magic shows. They were magical because they told stories that sprouted out of nowhere and because each ballet was always surprising: one minute was different from the next. As I grew older I came to understand that the stories did come from something tangible and that the surprises were calculated. Underneath their theatrical vitality was what I call in this book "craft." Still later on, as a critic, I took it as one of my jobs to describe as many aspects of this craft as best I could, not only because I admired them, but also because it gave me pleasure to ferret out the nuts and bolts of the larger design and purpose. What made it all beautiful to me was the ballet vocabulary itself. I was crazy about arabesques and quick little flutters of the feet and the silken line of the women's legs in pointe shoes. As a student of ballet, at the School of American Ballet, I grew to love the vocabulary even more, especially as I learned to respect the logic of how one exercise related to another.

What I experienced as a student rolled back onto Balanchine's stage, only a few blocks from where I studied. The choreography of his ballets—many of them, at least—had a surprisingly close relationship to the classroom, but with a difference. How close and yet how far! To this day, the tension between roots and their flowerings on stage fascinates and excites me. The same holds for the seemingly endless recombinations and permutations to which Balanchine subjected the rudiments of classical technique. This, too, is craft—and something more, for supporting his understanding of how to work basic materials over and over was his belief that this is a fine way to make art. It takes conviction, trust, and courage to pursue this approach through more than four hundred ballets. So I see Balanchine as a person of good moral fiber, and that also pleases me.

The magical part of Balanchine's art cannot be explained by craft alone. It concerns the relationship between music and dancing, a topic that is not much discussed in the essays that follow. A good deal has been made of the fact that he was a musician; thus, the reasoning goes, his technical knowledge of music accounts for the sublime synchrony between what you see and what you hear. That may be, but how to explain the emotional and spiritual resonance of so many of his ballets? I think it's because Balanchine listened to music with his imagination and that his mind was unusually receptive to the dynamics of music. All that was stirred in him he put in the ballets. This translation from inner to outer life is one aspect of his genius, but the desire to give his inner life a public forum took courage as well.

Balanchine used to say that you can't put dancing into words, that you can only look at it. The analytical side of me says, Balderdash! But the part of me that weeps and smiles when watching his ballets lays pen to rest. Balanchine is right.

Apollo

1928

Balanchine made *Apollo* in 1928, under the inspiration of Stravinsky's score and under the auspices of Diaghilev's Ballets Russes. He was all of twenty-four years old. As his oldest surviving ballet, and by general consensus one of his great ballets, *Apollo* has a biographical fascination. It offers a rare glimpse of his achievements as a young man, but in so doing inevitably raises questions. Was it his first great ballet? Were there intimations of *Apollo*'s so-called neoclassical style in earlier works? Was *Apollo* a continuation of what came before, or was it, as Diaghilev suggested, something new? Yet how could Diaghilev place it in dance history, for he had not seen the ballets Balanchine made before joining the Ballets Russes in 1925. And there were many of them. The official chronology of his work, which was compiled with his participation, cites 1920 as the beginning of Balanchine's choreographies. He was prolific from the get-go: *Apollo* was his eighty-fourth ballet, although many of these works were small, occasional pieces or divertissements for operas.

As young as Balanchine was when he made *Apollo*, there is a huge gap in the story of his early years. Was he a genius from the start? Reminiscences of colleagues from his student days in St. Petersburg describe his ceaseless flow of inventive ideas, the ease with which he worked, and his sensitivity to the individuality of his dancers, suggesting that he was indeed a prodigy. Young geniuses become mature geniuses if they're lucky, but does the idea of artistic development apply to Balanchine? My own opinion is that starting with *Apollo* he made ballets of varying quality, but that they yield no consistent line of development. Perhaps one can say the same of his pre-*Apollo* days.

I would guess that Balanchine's pact with the god of genius was a done deal from the time he first entered the studio as a choreographer, just like Terpsichore's claim to the title of the goddess of dance is clinched even before she performs a duet with Apollo, when she walks on stage and joins the tip of her index finger with Apollo's in a replication of Michelangelo's God animating Adam.

If Balanchine may have a say in all this speculation, he never called *Apollo* a great ballet or his first great ballet, but he did famously call it a "turning point" in his life. He wrote this in 1947 in an essay for the magazine *Dance Index*, in which he paid homage to Stravinsky as a composer for dance. He wrote, "In its discipline and restraint, in its sustained one-ness of tone and feeling, the score was a revelation. It seemed to tell me that I could dare not use everything, and I, too, could eliminate." He added, "It was in studying *Apollo* that I came first to understand how gestures, like tones in music and shades in painting, have certain family relations. . . . Since this work, I have developed my choreography inside the framework such relations suggest."

It's the second comment, about steps having familial relations, that gets to the core of Balanchine's genius as a craftsman. His intuitive grasp of which steps speak to each other and which do not, of the basic fact that steps have personalities, helps account for the remarkable coherence of each ballet, no matter how complex the music or choreography. In the end, a Balanchine ballet makes sense, and its feeling for the "familyness" of steps is what gives each ballet its unique signature.

Balanchine's comments about *Apollo* all point to the business of artistic mastery, of shaping and controlling one's material. It so happens that this is also the theme of the ballet. *Apollo* traces the god's life from birth to his ascension of Mount Parnassus. Throughout the ballet Apollo is testing the limits and capabilities of his body. Once he learns to walk (in the first scene), he wants to figure out how forcefully he can swing his arms and legs, how much flexibility is in his back—see how his torso contracts and arches in his first solos—how far he can lean backward without falling down. He experiments even with his hands—clenching them into fists, then opening them. (Balanchine got these open-and-close, on-and-off sequences from neon lights he saw flashing in Piccadilly Circus—or so the story goes.) He wants to know what makes the lute tick from top to bottom. He cradles

Maryinsky Ballet. *Left to right:* Igor Zelensky, Maya Dumchenko, Olga Yesina, Viktoria Tereshkina. *Apollo.* Choreography by George Balanchine © The George Balanchine Trust. Photo by © Costas.

it in seemingly endless positions. He looks at it from afar, close up. With a rambunctious windup, he strikes the lute's strings as though it were a banjo. Later on he makes a sound so soft, he must place his ear against the strings to hear it.

When Apollo dances with the three Muses he sports with them as though they were parts of a mobile, first partitioning the trio into groups of two and one, then shaping all three into picturesque poses. He partners them two at a time, one by one, in the air, into the ground.

Later on, he appraises them from a critic's point of view: each of the Muses dances a variation for him, a sort of audition in which they display their artistic wares. The first two, Calliope (goddess of poetry) and Polyhymnia (goddess of mime), goof up, and Apollo dismisses them—rather rudely, I would say. Terpsichore pleases the god and gets to dance a duet with him. Polyhymnia's mistake is obvious. She must be silent, and so dances her jaunty variation with a finger pressed to her lips. At the very end, though, she flings her arms toward the audience and opens her mouth—wide! She covers her mouth in shame and runs off like a naughty schoolgirl. Calliope's problem is harder to read. My understanding is that she keeps running out of ideas. She starts with big ones; that is, she clutches her bosom as though digging deep inside herself, and then declaims with stentorian arm movements. These grand (grandiose?) beginnings end with whimpers, her body sagging. So Apollo sends her packing too.

Because *Apollo* is not a literal narrative, it's not wise to look for specific reasons why Terpsichore's solo is the "best." But it's worth noting that hers is the most three-dimensional of the lot. If there is one salient characteristic of her solo, it's that she keeps revolving around herself, showing her body to the audience from all possible angles. She offers full disclosure. Decades later, in other ballets, Balanchine was still arranging his choreography so that the ballerina would be presented to us as fully as possible. Indeed, self-revelation is the definition of a Balanchine ballerina—and if you wish to extend the physical realm into a disposition of courage and honesty, please feel free. Naturally, Apollo brings Terpsichore back for a pas de deux, after he does a variation of his own. What I particularly love about his solo is its encoded homage to ballet technique. Accompanied by grand chords from Stravinsky, Apollo thrusts his arms skyward, as if holding up the world in the raised palms of his hands. But it's not his arms that give him Herculean strength; it's his legs locked tightly in fifth position. Fifth position, of course, is the cornerstone of ballet; it's the beginning and the end.

The pas de deux for Apollo and Terpsichore also refers to the source of life, by way of Michelangelo's fresco. But the grandeur of the encounter quickly gives way to less godly moods—playfulness, tenderness, friendly competition. These moods come and go with the breezes of a spring day, and they characterize the rest of *Apollo*.

At its premiere the ballet ran into trouble with the critics. The authenticity of the ballet's classicism was naturally a main bone of contention. Music critics thought the music a rehash of old material. Dance people were horrified by Balanchine's so-called distortion of classical principles. It's easy to find the sinning elements in the choreography—the occasional turned-in leg, the flat-footed shuffles, the novel ways of partnering, the inclusion of acrobatics. (My god! Was that Terpsichore doing the splits?) None of this stuff was new, but now it was applied to noble subject matter. After the premiere, a critic challenged Balanchine with this question:

"Tell me, Mr. Balanchine, where did you ever see Apollo on his knees?" To which Balanchine answered, "Tell me, Mr. So and so, where did you ever see Apollo?"

I think that it's the ballet's sportive, humanizing attitude toward mythological figures, rather than actual dance vocabulary, that was most unsettling for audiences in the 1920s; and to a certain extent contemporary audiences are still puzzled by the ballet's stance. Is it appropriate to smile? There are so many delightful bits. Think of the way Apollo struts his stuff after he has danced with Terpsichore, when he hoists two of the Muses with his arms. Or the way the Muses commandeer him when they lead him in the so-called troika. Apollo can barely contain their exuberance. Nor can any one of them resist Stravinsky's dance beat in the next-to-last scene, when they bounce up and down in time to the music. Merrill Ashley remembers that when she was in the corps she and some friends would gather backstage when the bouncing music arrived and have their own private bouncing session. That's how deeply Stravinsky can rouse the instinct to dance.

Apollo has moments of tenderness, too. Terpsichore courts Apollo when she offers him her palms on which he rests his head. That same gesture is repeated when, just before the god hears his destiny calling to him via Stravinsky's music, the Muses march up to him, clap their hands, and more or less insist that he rest for a while on their palms. My own favorite moment comes toward the end of Apollo's first dance with the Muses. They stand on pointe in a line with their heads thrown back, so that they cannot see what's in front of them. Apollo gives them a push, and off they *bourrée* into the world like children leaving home. It's time to grow up. Apollo gives each of them an object signifying their respective arts, and each dances a solo for him.

By all accounts making *Apollo* was a happy experience for Balanchine and Stravinsky, and, more importantly, the memory of it stuck. The two continued to work on ballets together, culminating with *Agon* in 1957, and the professional relationship flowered into a friendship that lasted until Stravinsky's death in 1971. Yet the creation of *Apollo* was not all a bed of roses for Balanchine. Because Serge Lifar, who danced the title role, was Diaghilev's lover, Balanchine had to give him the VIP treatment. As ballet master, Balanchine would have naturally expected to pick the cast for the Muses. For Terpsichore, he chose Alexandra Danilova, who was living as

American Ballet Theatre. *Left to right:* Cynthia Gregory, Martine van Hamel, Deborah Dobson, Michel Denard. *Apollo.* Choreography by George Balanchine © The George Balanchine Trust. Photo by © Costas.

his wife at the time. But Diaghilev insisted on Alice Nikitina, because a major patron of the Ballets Russes was her sugar daddy. Worse yet, shortly after the premiere Diaghilev ordered Terpsichore's solo cut, saying it was boring. Balanchine had the temerity to tell his boss that the problem was the dancer, not the choreographer. Soon after that scandal, the solo was restored and Danilova shared the role with Nikitina.

These kinds of conflicts were an affront to Balanchine's integrity and to his already-developed sense of his own worth. They were endemic, however, to the Diaghilev enterprise. This is not to say that Balanchine was itching to leave Diaghilev, but the impresario's death a year later, in 1929, was a liberation. Yet it did not resolve Balanchine's wish for artistic control. There were many more uncongenial situations to come, in Europe and in America, where he settled in 1933. It was not until 1946, with the creation of Ballet Society, that he finally achieved artistic independence.

The question is rhetorical yet inevitable: how many more of the ballets he made in Europe would have survived had he enjoyed greater institutional stability? (Keep in mind that until 1946 he was working as a freelancer.) In the field of dance, whether or not a ballet disappears is no measure of its worth. It's not a case of the survival of the fittest. On the other hand, once Balanchine had a steady company he dropped many ballets. So one can assume that the two ballets that have survived from the earliest years—*Apollo* and *Prodigal Son*—continued to find favor with their maker.

Prodigal Son has remained pretty much intact. *Apollo* is a different story. In 1979, on the occasion of Mikhail Baryshnikov's debut in the ballet with the New York City Ballet, Balanchine cut the prologue and first solo. He also changed the end. Gone were Apollo's birth, the presentation of the lute (given by handmaidens in ceremonial if unorthodox fashion—in a configuration dubbed "wheelbarrow"), and Apollo's dramatic pirouettes out of his swaddling clothes and first, wobbly baby steps. The brevity of the cut music, two or three minutes, belies the amount of information contained in the prologue. In the original ending, or apotheosis, the god and his Muses climb a staircase to Parnassus. With their arms floating upward and their front legs stretched forward on the ascending steps, they convey an incredibly moving sense of aspiration and limitless horizons. In its place, Balanchine inserted the famous "sun god" image—in arabesques, the Muses' legs radiate outward from the side of Apollo like rays of light. It's a magnificent image, but we have already seen it in the first version, moments before the climb up the staircase. Thus, the new version adds nothing new; it only subtracts. And by featuring this picturesque pose, one of *Apollo*'s many photo ops, in so prominent a position, Balanchine created something too close to what the late critic Robert Garis called "an *Apollo*-logo."

Quite apart from the musical issue—a "decapitation" of Stravinsky, as critics have come to call it—you can tell that I don't like what Balanchine did to his eldest child. I don't think anyone does. Sensitive to this feeling, some companies are allowed to present the ballet in toto. The question, of course, is why he did it. Balanchine never answered those who asked outright, except to reply crankily that *Apollo* was his to change. Perhaps it was a perverse reaction to the sacred status that the ballet had by then achieved—an urge to desecrate a holy site.

All one can say is that here is one instance where Balanchine made the wrong choice. But once he was rethinking it, why didn't he change a few other things that, to my eyes at least, could use fixing? I'm thinking of those flat-footed shuffles that Apollo and the Muses make. Or the Muses' hops to the side of the stage after they receive their emblems. Why not simply walk? Does Apollo downright fuss with his lute when he holds it every which way? Maybe one or two fewer maneuvers might have made the same point with more elegance. All of these "errors" show a Balanchine overly intent on inventiveness, on not living up to the less-is-more lesson he says he learned from working with the music.

In the end, though, as much as I abhor the big changes Balanchine made to *Apollo*, so do I cherish the minor flubs. They show that in 1928 Balanchine was a genius—a young genius.

Prodigal Son

1929

Had Balanchine choreographed *Prodigal Son* in, say, 1939, in the United States, he might have begun the ballet with a brief variation for the two servants: the opening bars of Prokofiev's score are just right for some vigorous movement. But the ballet was created in 1929, for Diaghilev's Ballets Russes, and so it begins with the two servants moving jugs and horns around instead of themselves.

The emphasis on props is just one reason why this piece looks like a Diaghilev production and not so much like a characteristic Balanchine ballet. Unlike *Apollo*, which predates it by a year, the choreography does not play off and against the classical principles of Petipa. There is no classical dancing in *Prodigal Son*. Imagine Balanchine devising a solo for a woman on pointe without making reference to an arabesque. Well, there are no arabesque-like figures for the Siren, and although there are *bourrées*, they are done with feet parallel. Pointe work, which is so central to post-*Prodigal* ballets, is irrelevant here. The reason the Siren wears pointe shoes is to give her additional height so that she may tower over her prey.

Just as central to the uniqueness of the ballet in the Balanchine canon is that, although there are fabulous dance moments—the pas de deux and the Son's variations—they are not crucial to the ballet's impact. Narrative points are as important as dance points. The opening scene contains the Son's most thrilling and extended variation, but one could argue that the moment when the Son stops dead in his tracks upon the entrance of his father, or the passage in which the father presses the boy's head down, demanding proper respect from his rebellious child, are as vivid and memo-

New York City Ballet. Mikhail Baryshnikov, Susan Freedman, and Shaun O'Brien (the father). *Prodigal Son.* Choreography by George Balanchine © The George Balanchine Trust. Photo by © Costas.

rable as the Son's leaps. And, of course, the most memorable scene of all, when the boy crawls home to his family, has no dance movement.

Considering that Balanchine made more than four hundred works, it is stupid to call any one ballet unique. Dancing is even less important in a piece like the 1947 *Renard* (which was reconstructed a few years ago by Todd Bolender) than it is in *Prodigal*. And as for the tortured acrobatics in the *Prodigal* pas de deux, they return in *Bugaku* (1963) and *Stravinsky Violin Concerto* (1972). Even so, it still makes sense to call *Prodigal* a very special ballet. The question is, how special would it seem to those who had seen Balanchine's earliest work, and who had witnessed the cultural scene in which he grew up during the early 1920s in Russia, before he immigrated to the West?

Prodigal Son, although his second oldest surviving ballet, was number ninety-four. That's a lot of choreography under the bridge. One of the fascinations of the ballet is that it opens a window on what the young Georgi Balanchivadze was up to. Written accounts of that time are scant and vague, but they all mention the inventiveness of his duets and their erotic nature. Some were acrobatic, a quality that did not always win approval. Wrote one critic in 1924 of an unnamed Balanchine ballet:

> I've lived for thirty years, o gods divine,
> And never knew until today
> That to break one's legs and spine
> Is a search for a new way.

Possibly, what strikes us as bold and startling in the *Prodigal* duet was actually old hat, a reworking of many earlier duets. Some critics found that Balanchine sometimes pushed too hard for the bold and startling. You can see that striving in *Apollo*, but less, I think, in *Prodigal*, although I sometimes wonder if he might have been less unrelentingly interesting in the duet had he created it when he was older. One also detects an overabundance of imagination in the dance for the drinking companions. I am thinking of the moment when Balanchine sets them in the design of a wheel. Because he breaks the momentum of the dance to get them into the wheel figure, it seems an insertion, a bright idea stripped of its musical context. The wheel image, however, sheds light on the cultural ideology in which Balanchine grew up and which he met again in the Ballets Russes.

Presenting man as machine was a favored way of glorifying in art the industrial age. The Russian scholar Elizabeth Souritz, speaking at a Balanchine symposium at the University of Michigan in 2003, conjectured that Nikolai Foregger's "machine dances" may have been in Balanchine's mind when he made *Prodigal*. Another Diaghilev ballet, the 1927 *Pas d'acier*, was devoted to the man-as-machine metaphor. The Constructivist movement, although more influential in architecture and the visual arts, also made an imprint on *Prodigal*, particularly in its use of the celebrated wooden fence. Functional as well as decorative, the fence becomes a banquet table, crucifix, boat, and fence once more.

The desire to bring industry and art, the functional and the decorative, under one tent extended to making an amalgam of beautiful and ugly movement, and high and low art—that is, dance and circus. During his student days in Petrograd, Balanchine worked in cabaret theater as a

New York City Ballet. Edward Villella and the drinking companions. *Prodigal Son*. Choreography by George Balanchine © The George Balanchine Trust. Photo, Jerome Robbins Dance Division, The New York Public Library for the Performing Arts, Astor, Lenox, and Tilden Foundations.

dancer and choreographer. He saw and performed in experimental ballets on the concert stage. He played piano as accompaniment to silent movies. In short, he was all over the place. So it should be no surprise that circus stunts found their way into the pas de deux of *Prodigal*, and that grotesquerie should be prominent in his choreography for the drinking companions, who, in Balanchine's words, "are absolutely awful."

Balanchine said it was his idea to make them bald. But the basic scheme of the ballet and selection of collaborators fell, obviously, to Diaghilev and Boris Kochno. Diaghilev wanted a ballet with a religious theme but with a simple libretto. Kochno suggested the story of the prodigal son from St. Luke's Gospel and pared it to the bone: boy has everything, boy has nothing, boy has everything again. Diaghilev chose Prokofiev to compose the music, which he did with a speed that made Diaghilev uneasy but that eventually pleased him. He wanted Matisse for the décor. When he declined, Kochno suggested Rouault, who readily accepted the commission even though he had never worked in the theater. Casting was a no-brainer: Lifar as the Son and the long-legged Felia Doubrovska as the Siren.

Work proceeded smoothly, with just a few crises. Rouault, for example, watched rehearsals eagerly, ate good lunches and generally enjoyed the high life in Monte Carlo, but came up empty-handed whenever Diaghilev asked to see sketches of the décor. One afternoon Diaghilev arranged for him to take a long drive along the Riviera, during which time he stole into Rouault's hotel room to find the sketches. He found nothing. That evening he handed Rouault a train ticket back to Paris, and the next morning the artist appeared with a full portfolio of pastels in hand.

Shortly before the day of the premiere, on May 29, 1929, in Paris, Prokofiev wrote additional music for the Siren and drinking companions after they have robbed the Son. Balanchine quickly added the scene in which the fence transforms into a boat, with the Siren at the helm. My theory is that Diaghilev felt that more music was needed to convey the passage of time between the Son's physical collapse and his arrival home. This quickly arranged choreography has always looked dull to me. Indeed, much of the choreography for the drinking companions is weak. I think they posed a problem for Balanchine. Their moral degeneracy needed to find its equivalent ugly, mindless movement—not Balanchine's strong suit. What to do with them? Balanchine had one great idea—imagining them as insects—but a second or third image never materialized.

As Balanchine was quickly assembling action for this additional music on the day of the premiere, Lifar took to his bed, unable to get up. Just before curtain, however, he roused himself, having had an epiphany that the ballet was an allegory about him. "I am the Son," he declared, and hotfooted it to the theater. He scored an unqualified success.

Balanchine's feelings about his hit ballet were more ambivalent. He is on record as saying that Prokofiev was a nasty, ungenerous man and that Rouault would never say a word to him. He chafed at being under Diaghilev's authoritarian rule. And if performance history means something, it is worth noting that Balanchine did not revive the ballet until 1950, casting the very fine actor/dancer Jerome Robbins in the title role.

Obviously it is a plum role in the male repertory, and it gives the dancer a plum challenge: how to find a balance between dance and naturalistic, psychologically motivated gesture. The difference between the two is perfectly illustrated by comparing the performance Baryshnikov gave in Chicago in 1975 and the one he recorded for television three years later, this time with the City Ballet under Balanchine's supervision. On the earlier occasion he often moved as the spirit moved him rather than in time to the music. In the later performance his gestures were as detailed and convincing, but they were controlled by Prokofiev's meter rather than by his own impulses. The misguidedness of the first and rightness of the second were especially apparent in the final scene, when the Son crawls toward his father. Emotion is powerful in proportion to the degree to which it is shaped by artifice. Otherwise, it's just ham.

Lifar, in later years, was often accused of chewing the scenery. Thus, it is all the more interesting to read that in rehearsals for *Prodigal Son* Diaghilev continually urged him to loosen up emotionally. Presumably he did, for the audience was moved to tears by the ballet.

Today, I think, audiences love the ballet for the same reasons they did in 1929. The Siren is a compelling mixture of hot and cold. "Reptilian," is how Edward Villella, a great Prodigal Son, describes her, and Doubrovska was particularly admired by contemporaneous commentators for embodying the paradox. The Son's story is told with great care. And the final scene—so noble and tender—speaks to our most human selves. I have a friend who back in the 1960s, when she was living in New York, found it difficult to cry when she was blue. Her solution was to go to the New York City Ballet to watch Villella dance the Son. As the curtain fell, she'd sit in her seat with tears streaming and face beaming.

Serenade

1934

Once he was in the United States, Balanchine lost no time in resuming his life as a choreographer. Under the auspices of Lincoln Kirstein, a modestly wealthy intellectual and patron of the arts, Balanchine had emigrated from Europe in the fall of 1933. On January 1, 1934, the School of American Ballet opened in New York—the location chosen after he had rejected Hartford, Connecticut, as home base—and in March he was already at work on *Serenade*, set to Tchaikovsky's *Serenade in C for Strings*. Kirstein, who kept a diary, wrote that before the first rehearsal, Balanchine told him that his mind was a blank and asked Kirstein to pray for him. It was Balanchine's practice, if anecdotal information is true, to commune privately with the ghosts of composers to whom he was choreographing. For Balanchine to ask a mere mortal for his good wishes was out of the ordinary.

Today, *Serenade* has great historical significance because it is the first ballet Balanchine made in America. Perhaps it had that significance for him as well. Would New York become a fruitful place for him to work? It must have been a pressing question, because in 1934 Europe was pretty much closed to him.

When Diaghilev died in 1929, after the premiere of *Prodigal Son*, the center of dance life collapsed. Having established a solid reputation as ballet master for Diaghilev, however, Balanchine was not at a loss for work; it's just that none of the opportunities panned out. He was commissioned by the Paris Opera to choreograph Beethoven's *The Creatures of Prometheus*, but two weeks after beginning work he developed tuberculosis. After recovering in the Alpine region of France, he returned to Paris, only to find that Serge Lifar had been hired in his place. Thence to London, where he contributed several dances for a theatrical revue produced by Sir Charles B. Cochran. In the summer of 1930 he was invited to be guest ballet master of the Royal Danish Ballet. The problem here was that the company wanted Balanchine to restage the old Diaghilev repertory; he wanted to make new ballets. Back, then, to London, where he did a few more dances for Cochran and Sir Oswald Stoll's variety show. The effects of the Depression had taken hold in the theater world by now, and with no jobs in the offing he could not have his residence permit extended.

Back to France. There, the highly cultured René Blum (brother of Léon Blum, the French Socialist leader) hired Balanchine to become ballet master of the new troupe he was forming, Les Ballets Russes de Monte Carlo. Things were looking up. Among the works he created for the troupe's debut season, in 1932, was one that was to become a famous "lost" ballet, *Cotillon*, starring the "baby ballerina" Tamara Toumanova. Blum's business manager, however, Colonel W. de Basil, was a rascal, and soon he and Balanchine were at odds. De Basil's high-handedness and ethical lapses—he was known to take bribes from would-be ballerinas—were anathema to Balanchine. He was pondering quitting when de Basil beat him to the punch and fired him.

The next opportunity came with Les Ballets 1933, a small troupe formed by Balanchine and dedicated to the principle of new, experimental work— that is, repertory not in the Diaghilev mold. The project was funded by Edward James. Their seasons in the summer of 1933 in Paris and London were not popular successes, and that was that. There was to be no Les Ballets 1934. So in the summer of 1933, when Kirstein, in London, proposed to Balanchine that he settle in the United States, the choreographer's response was all but predestined.

Fortunately for Balanchine, nostalgia for the good old days of Diaghilev did not rear its head in the New World as it had in the Old. Not that Balanchine had no use for the past; it's just that the past he admired was the classical ballets of Petipa and the academic language from which Petipa's ballets, and his own *Apollo*, had sprung. On the other hand, American dancers were not as well trained as Europeans. The students at the School of American Ballet, who were his live material for *Serenade*, were by and large rough-hewn and without stage experience. Thus, the creation of *Serenade* was informed by the necessity of making do with what was there.

What was there for the first rehearsal were seventeen students. With this uneven number, Balanchine could not arrange them in traditional order—say, four lines of four women. Instead, he set them in five diagonal lines—two lines of three women each, one line of five, and two more lines of three. This opening tableau is so beautiful that it always elicits gasps of pleasure from the audience. It should also be noted that this uneven number of dancers was bound to be problematic when it came time to divide the group into smaller clusters. So, shortly after the ballet begins one dancer slips off the stage into the wings. No matter. The point is that the celebrated opening moments of *Serenade* were dictated to some extent by chance. Other chance events also wound up as choreographic events. At one rehearsal, the most talented dancer in the group, Leda Anchutina, entered the studio late. It's in *Serenade*. On another occasion, a dancer slipped and fell. That, too, is in *Serenade*. I don't know at which point during the rehearsal the latecomer showed up, but Balanchine used the moment as a bridge between the end of the first movement, the Sonatina, and the beginning of the Waltz. That is, he took control of this chance event and placed it where it was structurally useful. Both accidents, it turns out, became dramatically significant as well.

Because the dancers were technically unpolished, Balanchine had to deploy them in a way that runs counter to his later ballets. Typically, he ordered his cast in hierarchical categories, a method he inherited from Petipa. In its simplest form, there is the ensemble and a lead couple. At its most developed, the ensemble is led by demi-soloists and the principals are backed up by soloists. One of the unique, and lovely, aspects about *Serenade* is the absence of a pecking order, at least in its earliest incarnations. As the years progressed, the solo parts were increasingly consolidated among fewer dancers. But even today there are many remnants of the original plan. You can see it right at the beginning, when two women emerge out of the group to make little runs around their neighboring dancers. The opening section especially is full of such fragmentary solo outings, making it difficult to isolate the big parts from the smaller ones. This is an extraordinarily unusual "problem" in a Balanchine ballet, but one that gives *Serenade* its feelings of community and sisterhood, and a fluidity equal to Tchaikovsky's lyricism.

Balanchine increasingly gave more weight to fewer dancers as more

New York City Ballet. Susan Pilarre. *Serenade*. Choreography by George Balanchine © The George Balanchine Trust. Photo by © Costas.

proficient dancers came along who could handle the demands of a full-fledged soloist part. The first production had no soloists, but nine prominent parts. At one point, in the early 1940s, one woman took the majority of soloist work. In later years five women assumed the solos, and today there are three. As you can imagine, the few men studying at SAB in the first *Serenade* must have had little partnering experience. One assumes this from the primitive bit of supported movement he made for four men in the Elegy. (Curiously, he never spruced up these few minutes in later versions.) The Waltz was first a dance for five women and an ensemble. Not until 1941 did Balanchine change the beginning of it to a proper pas de deux. In the same year he also added the so-called Russian Dance. This is the last movement of the score and so ends with rousing finality. It always draws applause from the audience, who assume that the ballet is over. But it isn't. Balanchine switched the Russian Dance from the last movement to the third, so that the ballet could end on a sad note, with the Elegy.

The closing passage of *Serenade* is indeed elegiac. A woman rushes toward another with outstretched arms, embraces her, and falls to the ground. Four men appear. She peers up at them. They somberly lift her on their shoulders and carry her toward the back of the stage. Her arms stretch toward the sky higher and higher, and a cortege of women follows. As the curtain falls, the women's backs arch forward and their chests open to the heavens above.

There is some sort of story going on, the only questions being what and why. Every viewer has an interpretation. Speaking for myself, I believe that the woman is accepting her destiny, that she is Joan of Arc about to become Saint Joan, rising in flames toward heaven. Why the ballet has come to this moment I do not know, nor do I know why the Elegy opens as it does, with a woman guiding a man, blindfolded by her hands, toward the "Saint Joan" woman lying on the ground. (To this day I still can't figure out the source of the Saint Joan image, but I feel it in my bones.)

Again, a narrative of sorts is going on, but there is no motivation, depiction of character, or other characteristics of traditional narrative to tell us where we are. The things that happen in *Serenade* just happen. The ballet is a fantasy in the extreme. Some critics have said that Balanchine's way with narrative resembles modernist literature. In *Will in the World*, the Shakespeare scholar Stephen Greenblatt finds a similar method in Shakespeare's later plays. He calls it a "strategic opacity." In *Hamlet*, he writes, "Shakespeare found that if he refused to provide himself or his audience with a familiar, comfortable rationale that seems to make it all make sense, he could get to something immeasurably deeper," which was "an inward logic," a "poetic coherence." Greenblatt writes that Shakespeare "could provoke in the audience and in himself a peculiarly passionate intensity of response, if he took out a key explanatory element."

Serenade abounds with opacity. The why and wherefore of the beginning of the Elegy cannot be explained; it can only be absorbed and pondered. As I have written, a woman whose arms are entangled around a man leads him blindfolded toward the woman on the ground. Bound together in sculptural poses, the three dance. Other women come leaping at him, while he stands in the middle of it all, somewhat impassive. The action evolves into a passage for the man and three women—the three Fates? Then the story abruptly breaks off and moves into a formal, abstract passage for the entire ensemble. They exit, leaving us with the original grouping of the man and two women. The woman who has escorted the man across the stage stands behind him and presses her arms up and down, like angel wings. (She is often dubbed "the dark angel.") The strength of her arm movements and the declamatory chords in the music suggest that a turning point has come.

National Ballet. *Top to bottom:* Michele Lees, Kevin McKenzie, Christine Knoblauch. *Serenade.* Choreography by George Balanchine © The George Balanchine Trust. Photo by © Costas.

She leads the man off, leaving the woman on the ground prostrate. It's at this point that she rushes into the embrace of the woman with outstretched arms, which sets the scene for the ballet's conclusion.

Always skittish about interpreting his work, Balanchine was sometimes more, sometimes less giving with his ideas. He called *Serenade* "a dance in the moonlight." He used words like "fate" and "destiny." To Alexandra Danilova, who was once in *Serenade*, he gave an amusingly specific explanation of it all. Danilova reports, in Francis Mason's *I Remember Balanchine*, "The girl in the ballet who leads the boy to the girl who lies on the floor is his wife. I asked Balanchine who she was and he told me this. She is his wife and together, he said, they pass down the road of life. I, the girl on the floor, was pitied by the man, but I was a frivolous girl who had one affair after another. Then I was left alone."

Well, so much for opacity and so much for Saint Joan. Possibly, Balanchine was still mad at Danilova for leaving him when they were living together in Paris. Ecco: *Serenade* as morality tale.

Serenade's opacity enters the ballet much earlier than the final, Elegy section. Toward the end of the first, Sonatina movement, a woman enters the stage, which is filled with the ensemble in their opening formation. (Presumably, she is the girl who came to rehearsal late.) She wanders among them, seemingly looking for her place, which she eventually finds. The moment is in stark contrast with the general ebb and crest of the preceding action, because there is nothing general about what she is doing. She is lost, and then with the beginning of the Waltz, she is claimed by a man who walks toward her on a diagonal as the ensemble leaves the stage. The lost woman is telling us a story out of the blue, while the man who approaches her foreshadows the long walk of the man and dark angel in the Elegy section. Without wanting to push the images too far, I believe there is a correspondence between the layering of events in *Serenade* and the "poetic coherence" Greenblatt describes in Shakespeare. However mysterious and inexplicable *Serenade* is, it feels right and of a piece—this despite the fact that it was a work in progress for so many years.

My mother once told me that when I first started going to see the New York City Ballet as a child, I couldn't believe that a person had actually made the ballets. I thought they were aspects of nature, like blue skies and green grass and rain. It must have been *Serenade* that put this notion into my head. Its patterns and rises and falls in momentum and crystallizations and dissolves are beautiful pure and simple—beautiful and poignant, poignant because they are so beautiful. As I grew older I came to realize that much hard work and artifice helped to achieve that beauty. Still, there is always dumb wonderment that a mere person could have dreamed up its loveliness.

Sometimes I think that *Serenade* must surely be my favorite ballet, but I equivocate: there is this one, and that one, and the other. I am reminded of an anecdote that Robert Craft told about Stravinsky. He asked Stravinsky who his favorite composer was. He said he couldn't reply because this composer had done this and that composer had done that. Craft pressed him for an answer. Finally, Stravinsky replied in a low voice, as if making a confession: Schubert. I think *Serenade* is my Schubert.

Concerto Barocco

1941

Considering the importance that music played in his artistic life, it's worth noting that Balanchine rarely chose to choreograph to the great pieces of musical literature. *Concerto Barocco*, set to the Bach Double Violin Concerto in D Minor, is an exception. He said that what most pleased him was *musique dansante*, and his typical examples were Delibes, Tchaikovsky, and Stravinsky. He set far more ballets to the latter two than to any other composer.

When thinking about what music he might use for the next ballet, he enjoyed switching gears from the one he had just finished. Variety and contrast were as important criteria for choices of compositions as were the composers themselves. In terms of musical structure, Charles M. Joseph in *Stravinsky & Balanchine: A Journey of Invention* says that Balanchine was drawn to the concertante form because the dialogue between solo instruments had an inherent drama he could express choreographically.

But beyond these two generalities and his allegiance to Tchaikovsky and Stravinsky, it's hard to ferret out significant patterns in his musical taste, although there is evidence of bias. He liked Bizet, Mendelssohn, Hindemith, Glinka. Post-Tchaikovsky Russian music found no favor. Of course, there is Stravinsky to refute this claim, but I believe Balanchine preferred his French rather than his Russian side. Generally, Balanchine was sympatico with French music; indeed, he organized a big festival honoring Ravel in 1975.

Few German composers passed through his hands, which leaves the standard "great music" out in the cold. Often called a Mozartian choreographer, he did only a few things to Mozart, explaining that he did not feel he could add anything to the music. Proving the rule are a handful of exceptions: the Brahms *Liebeslieder Walzer* and Piano Quartet No. 1 in G Minor (but given a quite different coloration by Schoenberg's orchestration in the ballet *Brahms-Schoenberg Quartet*), Mozart's *Divertimento No. 15* and *Symphonie Concertante*, Schumann's *Davidsbündlertänze*, and finally the Bach Double Violin Concerto.

Balanchine's response to the music was to give tit for Bach's tat. *Barocco* is perfection. To amuse myself, I once looked at a videotape of the ballet several times in a row, scouring it for a sag, or error in judgment. There were no sags, and just one moment that could arguably be called an error in judgment: when the ensemble *bourrées* in place as the violins quiver. Too imitative, I thought. Actually, the moment happens twice, and the second time brought a smile to my face. Smiling is not a bad thing to do, so perhaps the simultaneous quivering of strings and legs is not an error, but a joke, consciously made by Balanchine. I'm not sure, but I've decided to give him the benefit of the doubt. *Barocco* is perfection.

It is cast for an ensemble of eight women, two female principals who correspond to the two violins, and a man who partners the "first" violin in the second-movement adagio—"first" in quotes because the first principal dancer doesn't always follow the first violin. Almost always, but not always. This is to say that, as strict as the ballet is, it is not bound by Bach or by the dance language around which Balanchine organized himself. As a small example of this freedom, the large movements are all arabesques, in keeping with the very clean lines Balanchine wanted for this ballet. In the adagio, the ballerina does hardly anything *but* arabesque. Yet Balanchine inserts one attitude in the piece, in the adagio, just as it is about to end. That one image of a bent rather than straight leg is not startling, but it is an infraction alright. "Why not?" one can hear the perpetrator of the crime say, as he often said in defense of liberties taken.

A large example of Balanchine's musical independence also occurs in the adagio. The music is seamless, seemingly headed for an eternity of time. Balanchine expresses the feeling with a seamless pas de deux, epitomized by arabesques done over and over and over. At one point, however, he breaks the long continuous line by bringing back the second violin, sending the man off stage, and returning to the opening formations of the adagio, for the ensemble and two lead women. Then, after returning to the very beginning, he fast-forwards to where he left off. The second violin exits and the man returns so that the pas de deux can resume. The break is noticeable, of course, but it's not a disruption of the flow. Following the music's return to the opening theme, the ballerina is again lifted in high arabesques, and the sailing is smooth until the end.

You have to wonder what prompted Balanchine to devise this curious backward/forward sequence of events. One motivation is that he wanted to mark a special moment in the music, when there is a subtle, unusual shift in its harmonic structure—to what I'd call a "blue" mode—accompanied by a steady, pressing upward line in the solo violins. This haunting moment happens twice. The first time, Balanchine acknowledges it by bringing the high lifts in arabesque to a climax: the ballerina soars seven times without interruption. He marks the second time with greater boldness. He arranges the partnering in a showy manner (the only showy bit in the entire ballet): the man slides the woman down and forward so that her whole body practically skims along the floor; then she swoops up into a high arabesque. As she is sliding forward, the second violin enters and moves across the stage in the opposite diagonal, moving against the thrust of the couple. Their crossing paths set up a crosscurrent, a friction strong enough to give one goosebumps. In this way Balanchine creates a new kinetic quality to echo the music's special tonality. With the second violin now in play, the dancing reverts naturally to the opening passage.

This explanation is, of course, a theory, but one sure thing is that, for all the sublimity of the pas de deux, the entrance of the second violin and her progress across the stage is the most amazing moment of the second movement.

The adagio is indeed sublime, but it is not a pas de deux backed up by an ensemble. I cannot think of any other Balanchine work where the ensemble and principal couple are so interactive, where a sense of community is so palpable. One sees it from the start. The ballerina is repeatedly lifted over and through a line of women, and each time she passes through, the ensemble responds in small gestures. They bow their heads, lunge to the side, shift their weight from one leg to the other. These are small flourishes, but it's the smallness that gives intimacy to the action. Later on, the involvement between the couple and ensemble grows more theatrical. There are any number of Balanchine's famous daisy chains, starting out for three

New York City Ballet. *Left to right:* Delia Peters, Richard Hoskinson, Allegra Kent. *Concerto Barocco.* Choreography by George Balanchine © New York City Ballet. Photo by © Costas.

New York City Ballet. Conrad Ludlow and Gelsey Kirkland. *Concerto Barocco.* Choreography by George Balanchine © New York City Ballet. Photo by © Costas.

or four dancers, then developing into a grand daisy chain for everyone, where the group of ten weave themselves into a dense cluster, then about-face and unravel into two simple lines.

Typically, dancers, like regular people, make contact with their arms. In *Concerto Barocco* they say hello to each other with their legs. One dancer lunges deeply while another jumps over the extended leg. We have seen this in *Serenade*, where the extended leg beckons, as it were, the other dancer into a jump. In *Barocco* the movement is less suggestive, but it is certainly more prevalent. As in every idea in the ballet, Balanchine enlarges upon it until it reaches a final destination. The man and four of the women lunge in a line, while the ballerina must walk down the line and step over the fourth woman's leg without losing contact with her partner's hands. Will she make it? Sometimes it's a bit of a stretch.

Like the jump-over-the-leg motif, the dancing in *Barocco* carries less imagistic weight than in other ballets. What you see is what you hear; the music inspires Balanchine's powers of analysis, not his poetic sensibility. The approach resembles that of *Agon*, except that the pas de deux in *Agon* has much extramusical content. In *Barocco* the pas de deux is breathtakingly beautiful, but unlike almost all other Balanchine duets, it has no romantic overtones. Many observers have noted this special purity, and one reason is that Balanchine wanted to keep his mind on the score. Another reason, I think, for the absence of love feelings in the duet is that he was more interested in the family unit of ten than in the man/woman relationship.

The relationship between the two dancer-violins in the first and third movements is also determined by Bach. Just as the main themes pass with dexterity and grace between the two musicians in the pit, so do they move between the two on the stage. For the most part, but not always, the dancer soloists imitate phrases in canon, leaving the knottier structures to the musicians. In my memory, I had imagined that the two dancers moved in a tighter space in the last movement than in the first, but a check with reality (a video) revealed that the two move neck and neck in the first movement as well, yet not as much as in the original 1941 version. In a film that shows Marie-Jeanne, the original first violin, coaching young dancers from the School of American Ballet, she wanted them to dance even closer. "You should be in each other's way," she said.

Spacing aside, there is certainly a difference in the quality of their relationship. Their imitative dialogue in the first movement is harmonious, whereas in the third they "play" the central theme with different phrases of movement. The music they make together is thus more complex, with more thrust and parry and, depending on the dancers, a hint of competitiveness. In the late 1970s there was more than a hint of it when Suzanne Farrell and Kyra Nichols were the principals. Farrell was the reigning queen; Nichols, the up-and-coming soloist. Nichols's thrusts were aggressive, and rather than simply move progressively closer to Farrell, as the choreography demands, she seemed to be moving in on Farrell's territory. They were a thrilling series of performances.

What I love in the first movement is the way Balanchine manipulates a simple movement into a complex one, then turns it into the central image of the entire section. All the dancer does is overcross the leg that is pointed forward in *tendu*, then twists her torso into that leg. The result is a corkscrew design, rather baroque in its complexity. (In the 1941 version, the leg in *tendu* was bent, thus deepening the baroque look.) The dancers execute this step almost from the beginning of the movement, leading with one leg, then the other. The principals do the same thing soon after their entrances.

The step is catchy in itself, especially as the torsion it requires complements Bach's contrapuntal line. More delightful, though, are the endless variations Balanchine devises for his theme. The women move straight forward or on a diagonal, one group moves to the left while the other moves to the right; sometimes they and the principals do it in unison, sometimes on consecutive beats, as in a canon. Meanwhile, the second part of the theme alternates between little hops backward in arabesque or in a turned-in *passé*. You'd have to look hard to find a dance that is as focused on one idea as this one. Indeed, the motif is so famous that several choreographers have duplicated it as homage or parody. The audience always gets the reference.

The last section is not as motif-laden. I'd say it's the most exciting musically. This is the "bebop" section, with one group moving in a BE-bop accent while the other counters with be-BOP. The syncopation reaches its acme in another iconic moment: the women hop on pointe while their arms quickly move up and down on consecutive beats. As if this rhythmic teaser were not enough, Balanchine adds frosting by having the group hop into different patterns, like moving panels. These are moments of total joy, compounded by a bit of mathematical mysteriousness. What in hell are the musical cues that tell the dancers when to lower their arms and raise them again?

I have seen my fair share of *Barocco*s and was never able to figure it out. One day, Merrill Ashley led me into the inner sanctum of the passage and told me on which counts the dancers move. It's so simple, I'm embarrassed to pass it on to the reader as if it were classified material, but here it is anyway: one group lowers their arms on count three, and the other on count four. It's not easy to do, however. Just after Merrill revealed the secret code, I took the bus home and practiced my *ports de bras* en route. So engrossed, and confused, did I become in the project that I missed my bus stop by a mile.

One has to wonder how long it took Balanchine to think up that passage. Yes, he hears music well, but still . . . And ditto for the entire ballet. Its architectural elegance, musical acuteness, superb craftsmanship, and theatrical wizardry all imply that Balanchine thought about the music and what he might do with it for a long time. If he did, it must have been while he was sleeping. His waking hours around the time of *Barocco*'s creation, in 1941, were too hectic and far-flung for sustained thought. In 1941 he had no permanent company. He was leading not only a freelance life, but also a bicoastal one. The previous year he had been in Hollywood and working on a couple of musicals for Broadway.

The year 1941 was unique in that his focus was entirely on concert dance. In January he premiered *Balustrade* (to Stravinsky's Violin Concerto). Then he prepared eight ballets for a tour of Latin America, which began in June and which had been arranged by Lincoln Kirstein through his friend Nelson Rockefeller. Within about four months' time he created four new works as well as reviving four older pieces. Among the new works was *Concerto Barocco*. The other great one was *Ballet Imperial* to Tchaikovsky's Piano Concerto No. 2. Both ballets were shown in a public dress rehearsal in New York in May, along with Antony Tudor's *Time Table*, his first work made in America. *Concerto Barocco* officially premiered in Rio de Janeiro on June 27.

With their ruffled skirts for the ladies, Eugene Berman's costumes were appropriately Baroque in style. Nevertheless, they and the décor as well were discarded by Balanchine in 1951 in favor of simple practice outfits. In this first of the black-and-white ballets that Balanchine pioneered, the ladies wore black tunics and the man black tights and white T-shirt. In the early 1960s the women began wearing white tunics. This seemingly minor alteration did in fact change the entire look of the ballet, rendering it less geometric and more sculptural. At first, the change from black to white was disturbing for its softening effect. But now, some thirty-five years later, everything about *Concerto Barocco* is just fine.

The Night Shadow / La Sonnambula

1946

More than any other ballet in the Balanchine repertory, *La Sonnambula* rides on one section, the pas de deux between the Poet and the Sleepwalker. It is an extraordinary dance depicting an extraordinary situation. The Poet attends a masked ball, and when the guests later depart, a Sleepwalker slips onto the stage, her hand holding a lighted candle. She quickly runs around the ballroom, oblivious to everything. Yet the stalking quality of her steps suggests that she is propelled by an inner urgency. The Poet is immediately captivated by this sylphlike creature. He attempts to make contact with her, to possess her. He pulls her this way and that. He lifts her leg. He turns her. He lowers her body into a deep arabesque *penchée*. She acquiesces, yet without conscious recognition of his presence. She slips away from him—on purpose or not, we do not know—and continues on her path of *bourrées* as insistent as is her grasp of the candle she holds. Growing more desperate, the Poet tries to block her path. He extends his leg in front of her. She *bourrées* on. He lies down. She steps over his body—seeing it or not, we do not know—and *bourrées* on. Finally, when the music reaches a crescendo, he embraces her body and sinks to the floor in a tortuously achieved backbend. So extravagant is his gesture, it seems that he would lay down his life for her. She *bourrées*. He kisses her, and she exits.

The somnambulist is as much an enigma to the audience as she is to the Poet. Who is she and why has she entered the ballroom? Especially when she first appears, there is a fierceness to her steps, akin to the Wili Giselle's first solo in Act II, just after she has sprung from the grave. Although she skims the ground, the Sleepwalker doesn't waft about aimlessly. There is a specificity to her travels, yet we don't know if she is moving toward or away

New York City Ballet. Nikolaj Hubbe and Wendy Whelan. *La Sonnambula*. Choreography by George Balanchine © The George Balanchine Trust. Photo by © Costas.

from something, someone. At one point she rotates in sharp right angles, as if tracing the four walls of a room. The inner anxiety we sense in her—is she a captive? Am I getting too imaginative? Maybe. The point is that the tension between the Sleepwalker's outer impassivity and inner agitation is thrilling.

How unusual it is that a choreographer famous for directing his dancers to just do the steps relies in this ballet on a dancer's ability to project an inner life. He created the role in 1946 for Alexandra Danilova and the Ballet Russe de Monte Carlo. Under its original name, *The Night Shadow*, it was one of five new ballets he made for the company between 1944 and 1946 and the only one to have survived until the present day. Critics and dancegoers from the time remember the amazing intensity Danilova brought to the role. In my time, *the* Sleepwalker was Allegra Kent, whose fragility belied an inner turmoil made of iron. Her upset seemed frozen in time; her body, on the threshold of evaporation. Suzanne Farrell was

New York City Ballet. Allegra Kent. *La Sonnambula*. Choreography by George Balanchine © The George Balanchine Trust. Photo by © Costas.

also memorable for the sheer beauty of her presence. Even an indifferent Sleepwalker, however, cannot dilute the power of the pas de deux.

The rest of *La Sonnambula*'s choreography is middling. Much of the dancing is social dance and as such is of limited interest. What's surprising is that the opportunities for invention—the pas de deux for the Poet and the Coquette and the three divertissements performed to entertain the party guests—are middling as well, although the people who so loved Danilova also felt that Maria Tallchief, the Coquette in the original production, brought such sensuous energy to the role that she made the duet with the Poet important.

The score, based on several Bellini operas, and the libretto as well were created by Vittorio Rieti, a friend of Balanchine's. For me, it's the story and the ideas therein that keep me interested in the ballet as a whole. The Poet is almost as much an enigma as the Sleepwalker. Balanchine gives him a terrific entrance. He steps into the back corner of the ballroom and just stands there, with aristocratic mien and a touch of hauteur. The guests at the ball are chilled, yet fascinated by his stillness, his refusal to enter the room. In a kind of power play he forces the Baron, the host of the ball, to walk the length of the stage to greet him. The Poet obliges with a bow.

Looking past his host, his eye falls on the Coquette, and the Baron invites them to dance with the others.

The social dancing is interrupted when entertainers perform divertissements for the guests. When all leave, the Poet and Coquette peer into the wings to see if they are indeed alone, and they dance an amorous pas de deux. They are interrupted by a polonaise for everyone. As the couples parade off the Baron snatches the Coquette from the Poet, leaving him alone. Enter the Sleepwalker. After their duet the guests return and the Coquette, who has seen the Poet kiss the Sleepwalker, whispers in the Baron's ear. In a rage he storms off, and the Poet staggers on, fatally stabbed. The Sleepwalker enters and appears to grieve over the body. Four men carry his dead body to the Sleepwalker and deposit him in her arms. The ethereal woman carries him off (the *coup de théâtre* of the ballet), and as the curtain falls the guests look up and follow a glowing light as it travels across the upper reaches of the Baron's castle.

The conventional interpretation of the story is that the Poet aspires to an ideal and is killed for it, because the decadent society in which he lives cannot tolerate idealists. There's no question that the milieu he enters is decadent. The masked ball and the game of blind man's bluff the Poet is subjected to are traditional symbols of sexual license. Rieti's music has an uncomfortable dissonance, at times a sourness. And the stage action itself is disorienting, unpleasant. The guests speak in whispers, and the dances progress as a series of interruptions. Yet apart from his pursuit of the mysterious Sleepwalker, there is little to suggest that the hero has the soul of a poet. He is also drawn to the Coquette, and he does not reject her. It's just that someone more tantalizing comes along.

There is in the Poet an aspect of James, the protagonist of Bournonville's *La Sylphide*. (Perhaps it is no coincidence that three of the great Poets—Henning Kronstam, Peter Schaufuss, and Erik Bruhn, for whom Balanchine revived the ballet in 1960 for the City Ballet—are all Danes and had ample experience playing James before taking on Balanchine's Poet.) Like the Poet, James pays for being an idealist, but he is also destroyed because in seeking to enter the world of the sylphs he oversteps man's boundaries. The Poet commits the same sin, for the somnambulist inhabits something like a supernatural world not that far from the world of the sylph. *La Sylphide* is a morality tale pure and simple. The meaning of Balanchine's ballet is double-edged. The Poet is definitely a victim of an evil society and also personifies the loneliness of the artist as he struggles to pursue the unattainable. But in intruding on a party to which he is not invited and then picking off the ladies one by one—did he not have it coming to him?

The sleepwalking figure has a precedent in a Balanchine duet that was performed by Tamara Geva, his first wife, in 1924, called *Valse Triste* and set to Sibelius. According to Geva, as a sleepwalker she moved to the very front of the stage, raising the possibility that she'd fall into the orchestra pit. Some modern-day heroines of *La Sonnambula* also suggest that they're dancing on the edge of a precipice. The critic Arlene Croce finds that the entire ballet teeters on the edge, thus its troubling power. Generally, however, the many Balanchine works that take up the idea of the poet and the unattainable woman do not cloak themselves in Gothic chills. All Balanchine needs is an adagio tempo.

The story goes like this: the man has a vision, he and the vision dance a beautiful pas de deux, and then the vision departs, leaving the man alone with memory. The theme plays out in many variations. In *Serenade*, for example, the Dark Angel separates the man from the woman on the ground. This is his destiny. In *Le Baiser de la Fée* a long line of spirits come between the man and the woman. This, too, is man's fate. (One might say that it is woman's fate as well, were it not for the fact that earlier in the ballet it's the man who dreams and seeks.) The idea is worked out in highly theatrical terms in "The Unanswered Question" section of *Ivesiana*. In 1965, in his three-act *Don Quixote*, Balanchine focused on just one aspect of the Cervantes novel, the Don's quest for an ideal. In this ballet, however, the Don does not come up against destiny or fate as much as an evil society. Just as the little *Valse Triste* contained a kernel of *La Sonnambula*, so was *La Sonnambula* a prelude to the ideas expressed so eloquently, and morbidly, in *Don Quixote*.

Sometimes, though, it's not society or fate or the nature of human existence that makes life sad. Sometimes it's just that the beautiful adagio music comes to an end. I think especially of *Concerto Barocco*. Although it has no content beyond the interplay between music and dance, when at the very end of the adagio the man and woman bow to each other and exit in separate directions, one feels sad. Dance is ephemeral, and so is music. Whenever the adagio ends in a Balanchine ballet, life is sad, and there's nothing to be done about it except to move on to the allegro.

The Four Temperaments

1946

Serenade begins with the dancers' feet opening into first position. In *The Four Temperaments* two dancers lift their legs in a small *dégagé*. Perhaps it is mere coincidence that both ballets begin with a first-day-in-class exercise, but I like to think it was Balanchine's way of acknowledging each ballet's parallel place in his personal history. *Serenade*, the first ballet he made in America, was a fresh start. *The Four Temperaments* was also a fresh start, not only for himself but for Lincoln Kirstein.

After years in their respective diasporas—Balanchine on Broadway, in Hollywood, and as guest choreographer for various companies, and Kirstein running his own company and serving in World War II—the two reunited for a new project called Ballet Society, designed to put the Balanchine enterprise on more secure footing than it had ever enjoyed. *The Four Temperaments*, along with *L'Enfant et les sortilèges*, was on the first bill on November 20, 1946. Two years later Ballet Society became the New York City Ballet, and the story of Balanchine's wandering effectively ended.

Unlike *Serenade*, however, *The Four Temperaments* (commonly nicknamed *The Four Ts*) was a fresh start in two ways, institutionally and choreographically. After that little *dégagé* the dancers flex their feet, and because this is done in profile, it makes a doubly enormous impact. You can see—really see—the feet thrusting upward instead of pointing down into the floor, like they are "supposed" to. *The Four Temperaments* is famous for doing naughty things to classical line and normal partnering. And the fact that much of the dancing is done in profile heightens the effect of Balanchine's innovations.

Set to a commissioned score by Paul Hindemith, it begins with three

New York City Ballet. Jennifer Tinsley and Jason Fowler. *The Four Temperaments.* Choreography by George Balanchine © The George Balanchine Trust. Photo by © Costas.

duets (corresponding to the music's three-part theme) and then opens up into the four temperamental sections. Whereas the drama of the last four parts resides in its play on emotive qualities, the first part is most dramatic for its play with the academy. The knee, for example, is all but invisible in textbook ballet. It is prominent in *The Four Ts* from the start, when both of the dancers in the first duet move with one knee on the ground. It's just one step they take, but its slight awkwardness brings what could be a transitional move into high relief. Placing a woman on pointe with a bent knee is even more unorthodox, since the very point of dancing on pointe is to create a streamlined image. Balanchine develops the bent-knee motif as the three duets progress, starting with big *ronds de jambe*, moving to pirouettes, and finally to pirouettes in which the woman plunks her foot on top of her supporting bent knee.

The list of how Balanchine tweaks classical line is endless, but let me dwell a little on lifts in arabesque, since they are the means by which Balanchine achieves some of his most astounding effects. For one thing, sometimes the woman isn't lifted. She's dragged along the floor, which is how the first couple makes their exit. More often, Balanchine adjusts the arabesque into a frontal-view split. To add more fuel, he ends those splits with the woman straddled across the bent knees of her partner. We first see this maneuver in the second duet, and it is repeated over and over in the finale.

One can surmise that Balanchine really liked that one, but my own favorite adjustments to the aerial arabesque are the ones that the Sanguinic couple does. They are amazing, in part, because the man carries the woman at chest level rather than at full arm's height. Flying at such low altitude, and with a seamlessness that creates an illusion of slow-motion travel, the woman is an image of inverted power. She is capable not of mowing the world down, but of absorbing it into her own being. This in-gathering of energy is further heightened in her second tour of the stage, when the purposeful serenity of her travels is contrasted with the ensemble's staccato jabs and crouches. The four ladies go wild as they stab the floor in overdrive, but they don't deter Miss Sanguinic from keeping that front leg moving forward and up—calmly, inexorably.

Because *The Four Ts* looks at classical line with new eyes and in such thorough manner—the arabesques and bent knees are just starters—the ballet poses a question: Where did it all come from; are there antecedents? *Apollo* has plenty of "unballetic" moves, but they are less organic to the fabric of the ballet than are those to the fabric of *The Four Ts*. The dance writer George Jackson has said that its distortions may derive from Cubist painting. In recent years, scholars have pointed to African-American dance as a prime influence. They note the use of the pelvis as a fulcrum of movement and polyrhythms not only between groups, as in the Sanguinic variation, but also within the individual body, as in the Phlegmatic variation. They also note that Balanchine had worked on Broadway for many years with black dancers with various dance backgrounds, such as Josephine Baker, Katherine Dunham, and the Nicholas Brothers.

Brenda Dixon Gottschild, who has made the most comprehensive case for the "blackness" of *The Four Ts* in her book *Digging the Africanist Presence in American Performance*, finds a host of examples. Some are obvious—like the thrusting hips and polyrhythms—and a few are less so. For example, she compares the women alighting on their partners' thighs to a maneuver in the Lindy Hop. She also notes that the ending of the third duet, when the woman is dragged off by the man as she leans into his back, is often the way Lindy Hop couples exit the stage.

Even if every move in *The Four Ts* could be traced to a black or other nonballetic influence, however, the ballet has a sense of measure, deliberateness, and cohesiveness that one associates with classicism in its generic meaning. Indeed, the great paradox of *The Four Ts* is that despite the pulling and twisting of classical ballet it is one of Balanchine's purest examples of classicism. The clarity of each step—and the feeling of each as an inviolate entity utterly complete in itself—makes a deeper impression than the bent knees, pelvic thrusts, and so forth. Every second counts. Is there any transitional moment? I daresay not.

Nor are there any loose ends. If you imagine a classical painting, each object and shape finds its complement somewhere else on the canvas. A dance, of course, has far wider boundaries, spatial and temporal, than a painting, but even so, in *The Four Ts* the process of follow-through is extremely rigorous. I've already noted how this happens in the first three duets, but many of these moves travel through the ballet, picking up additional steam as they come to express the ballet's thematic content.

The *rond de jambe*, for example, is at first merely provocative, because the woman does it on a bent leg. When the Sanguinic ballerina repeats it, the movement suggests a revving up for her incredible trip around the stage. And the even more awesome journey, in the apotheosis, is also predicated on the *rond de jambe* of the Choleric figure, whose circles on the ground seem to clear the decks for the great, final launch into the stratosphere.

Another signature of the ballet is the pelvic thrusts forward and backward. After their introduction in the first duets, they carry through into the Melancholic, Phlegmatic, and Choleric sections, where they take on, respectively, aspects of menace, playfulness, and exaltation.

And so for all the radical look of *The Four Ts*, its tidy structure makes it easy to read. The ballet's content, however, is less accessible. To what degree is *The Four Ts* about the four temperaments? A dancer in the first production remembers Balanchine asking the cast if they knew what they were supposed to be. Worms? Bugs?, one of them pondered. No, Balanchine declared, then added rather grandly, "You are temperaments." But that's as far as the explication went.

Well, the Melancholic variation is fairly straightforward, although I personally would not describe the man's condition as sad, despite all the collapses to the floor. His main problem is that he can't get anywhere, can't get out of his own body. And when he's not thwarting himself, the ensemble of six women does the job for him. Two of the ensemble literally block his space, while the other four press in on him with their big *battements* and strong pelvic thrusts.

The Sanguinic section stands alone for its spatial amplitude. Picking up the short allegro section in the second duet, Sanguinic has a fair amount of fast dancing. It's also the most classical looking part of the ballet—for the lead couple at least. (The ensemble reminds me of Indians on the warpath in one section.) But do these qualities make the Sanguinic section cheerful, confident? Umm . . . In their ability to move freely, the Sanguinic couple are certainly a far cry from the Melancholic man who likes to enwrap himself in himself. On the other hand, see how easily the sanguine mood tips into choler. I write this because much of the choreography for the Sanguinic woman is replicated in Choleric's solo but heated up, "angrified." Yes, the Choleric woman is definitely full of big statements. The ambiguity of this section is carried by the four men and then four couples who attend her. Sometimes they seem to mock her (a feeling reflecting particularly strong agitation in the music). But at other times, again corresponding to the music and its repose, the four couples surrounding Choleric seem to calm her—perhaps to bless her—with their slow descents into arabesque.

Whereas the attendants of Choleric are both devils and angels, the ensemble women in Phlegmatic seem to be playmates of the leading man. But what is a stolid, impassive sort of guy doing with playmates; what does the phlegmatic temperament have to do with play? Nothing, and yet the Phlegmatic section strikes me as being primarily about play. While the legs of the Melancholic women create an obstacle course to which the man succumbs, the dancers in Phlegmatic turn those crisscrossing legs into a game of peek-a-boo. And the Melancholic man's collapses into heaps of woe are playfully mocked by Phlegmatic's imitation of him as a codger full of arthritic aches and pains. The stark angularity of the "Egyptian" arms in the first duet becomes in Phlegmatic almost a satire of fashion-model ennui

New York City Ballet. Jean-Pierre Bonnefoux in Phlegmatic. *The Four Temperaments*. Choreography by George Balanchine © The George Balanchine Trust.
Photo by © Costas.

(and forerunners of the *ports de bras* in the nonsatiric *La Valse*). Or they're
just plain weird. And talk about weird: How about that bit when the man
wraps his hand under his heel and hoists it up to his chest? Why does he
do this? Just to be weird, I think.

Phlegmatic's spirit of eccentricity reminds me of a description Alexandra
Danilova once wrote of Balanchine when they were living together in
France during the Diaghilev years. She wrote of his fey whimsy, of his
fondness, for example, of walking around their apartment wearing large
posters hanging around his neck, in the manner of the ballet *Parade*. If you
will permit me a weird thought, maybe Phlegmatic is a self-portrait of his
fanciful mood.

Here is another fanciful idea, about the connection between the ballet's content and the costumes. The costumes that Kurt Seligmann created for *The Four Ts* have traditionally been scorned for trying to steal the show from the choreography, a motive to which Seligmann readily admitted. From what one can see of surviving photographs, he turned the dancers into gargoyles. Some dancers wore helmets. Sanguinic was adorned in rags and bandagelike wrappings. One critic wondered if Phlegmatic was a mushroom.

Seligmann had a special interest in occult religion and black magic and obviously would empathize with the notion of medieval humors, the conceit upon which Hindemith built his score. It is possible to understand his costumes as perfectly reasonable visualizations of arcane bodily systems and his own private iconography of the mind. Of course the costumes were out of the question, and Balanchine began paring them down even before the curtain rose on the first performance. Yet there is something of their spirit in the choreography. The Phlegmatic section is a prime example. I also think that the Xs the dancers mark on the ground throughout the ballet, signifying something only the initiated could understand—and even the "Egyptian" arms—reveal Seligmann's influence.

By 1951, when *The Four Ts* entered the repertory of the New York City Ballet, Seligmann was banished. Good riddance, I suppose. Yet it would be fascinating to see the ballet with the costumes restored (well, perhaps remnants of them), in order to place the choreography's many secrets in fuller dialogue with what was a major component of the original conception.

Hindemith's score casts no such shadowy influence on the ballet. Even supposing that Hindemith subscribed to the idea of medieval temperaments, he believed more strongly in the idea of theme and variations, an idea that allowed Balanchine to make the magnificently cohesive edifice called *The Four Temperaments*. Moreover, the music's interplay between piano and strings inspired in Balanchine enthralling passages of syncopation and contrasts between strong movement (the piano) and pliable movement (the strings). Finally, the stately, temperate way in which the notes unfurl allows the choreography its measured control, its unhurriedness—the qualities that make the ballet classical.

Commissioning music is a gamble, and Balanchine rarely took the chance throughout his career. Apart from the Stravinsky commissions, the

Hindemith was one of his rare lucky hits. Although it would stand to reason that Balanchine was familiar with his music, it is worth noting the possible good word of Stravinsky, who admired Hindemith's work and was also his friend. (It was Hindemith who advised Stravinsky on how to expand the dimensions of violin technique for Stravinsky's good friend, the distinguished musician Samuel Dushkin, for a proposed violin concerto.) In 1937 Balanchine asked Hindemith to write something for piano and strings, about a half hour long, which Balanchine wanted to produce the following year. Hindemith suggested a ballet called *The Land of Milk and Honey*, but doubted he could have it ready by 1938. The commission was scrapped.

In 1940 Hindemith's agent called Balanchine to find out if he was still interested in a ballet. If so, he could deliver the first part in a week's time. During these years, it was Balanchine's custom to have musician friends over to his apartment in New York for informal musicales. At one such gathering the first part of what was to become *The Four Temperaments* got its first airing. Among the violinists were Nathan Milstein and Dushkin. The viola was played by Leon Barzin, who was to become the conductor for Ballet Society and the New York City Ballet. Balanchine's friend from the old days, Nicholas Kopeikine, played piano, and Edvard Fendler conducted. (Balanchine, I assume, played host.) The score was completed in 1940, and Balanchine wanted to produce it in 1941 for a possible tour of Latin America, the same tour for which *Concerto Barocco* was created. Pavel Tchelitchev, a friend of Kirstein and a previous collaborator with Balanchine, was asked to decorate the ballet, now called *The Cave of Sleep*. He imagined such an elaborate and expensive concept that the project was dropped. (His designs now reside at the Museum of Modern Art in New York.)

The Cave of Sleep slept for six years, when it emerged with the title we know today. It was very well received, but if there is a touch of the legendary about its premiere, it has more to do with the circumstances in which it was presented than with the ballet itself. In keeping with Ballet Society's plan to avoid the commercial world, Kirstein hired the auditorium of the Central High School of Needle Trades, a depressingly spartan place. Because the hall had no pit, Barzin and his orchestra worked on the stage itself, thereby adding insult to the injury already inflicted by the costumes.

Happily for all of us, audience and critics saw through the clutter to the thing itself, and *The Four Ts* has been with us ever since.

But with an important question: How easily did Balanchine's new-minded choreography materialize? Scattered memories of the original cast suggest that the process was more laborious than was typical for him. Because Balanchine had limited access to studio space, as was often the case, he worked on it in small increments, but a few dancers recall that he sometimes stopped the rehearsal even though there was more time, suggesting that he needed to think more before inventing the steps. He also jumped around from section to section more than usual. The scattershot process makes extraordinary continuity of movement motifs all the more remarkable.

Finally, the origins of the score itself are not completely known. Possibly, parts of what became *The Four Ts* were originally composed for a projected ballet by Massine, to be based on paintings by Breughel. Ideas from *The Land of Milk and Honey* may also have found their way into *The Four Ts*. Granted this is a long shot, but to my mind there is a connection between the title of the 1937 idea and Balanchine's galvanic conclusion to the ballet—with the ensemble's ground swell of power sending the principals into fearless flight. The country Balanchine's ballet describes is a cousin of milk and honey; it is the land of the free and the home of the brave.

Theme and Variations

1947

Toward the end of the polonaise section in *Theme and Variations*, all thirteen couples dash into place to form a long diagonal, and after a breath's pause they break into the polonaise step and tour the stage in a circle. I think it's the pause, that second of stasis, and then the release that takes your breath away. You sit back and think, Oh yes, this is it. What "it" is is hard to put into words. So let's borrow Ballet Theatre's phrase—"ballet in the grand manner"—which is how the company described the kind of ballet it wanted when it commissioned Balanchine to create one in 1947. Recommended to Balanchine by Ballet Theatre's music director, Max Goberman, the music is the last movement, "Tema con variazione," of Tchaikovsky's Suite No. 3. It premiered in November 1947 and starred Ballet Theatre's two reigning dancers, Alicia Alonso and Igor Youskevitch.

It's not only the largesse of that polonaise parade that makes it "the moment." It's a sense that we've arrived at the point of destination, for the entire section builds to that moment, mirroring Tchaikovsky's ascending line of excitation. How Balanchine keeps the dance action surging forward and upward is, to me, the chief glory of *Theme and Variations*, because underlying the drama of expectation and gratification is plain old craft.

The first thing Balanchine does to start the engine going (and to acknowledge the first of many drum rolls in the score) is to introduce men. The preceding sections are danced by women plus the male principal. Rather than have all twelve couples enter at once, he parcels out their entrances. Two enter, then two more, the third couple, and the fourth. To signal the first appearance of the polonaise melody, the four demi-soloist couples rush on and occupy stage center, giving them a special weightiness, which is underscored as they polonaise forward. The whole cast then follows their lead in the polonaise step. The second and third polonaises retreat slightly in force, as Balanchine substitutes variety of pattern for brilliance. One of the formations is a star; the other, crisscrossing lines. And to keep the polonaise step light and surprising, the dancers sprinkle in quick turns and jumps—those little flourishes that quicken one's pulse. Then, finally, the long diagonal of the entire cast, with the lead couple joining the polonaise for the first time. Doris Humphrey in *The Art of Making Dances* states that the diagonal is the strongest design the choreographer has at his disposal. I think she's right. And given the complex patterns that immediately precede the lineup, the simplicity of the diagonal is all the more powerful. It's the final resolution.

This moment does not end the ballet, however. It is actually followed by the finale, where everyone dances in unison, a device Balanchine used often to bring the stage to a crescendo. Curiously, though, for all the thrills and chills of choreography and music, it seems to me a postscript.

A crowd-pleaser throughout, for its gorgeous music and abundance of tutus as well as for its glamorous choreography, *Theme and Variations* offers any number of favorite moments for the audience, but it also has a particularly famous passage. This is the solo for the cavalier. All it is is a series of *ronds de jambe en l'air* on a diagonal, followed by another series of jumps across the front of the stage. Then the man runs to the back of the stage and completes his variation with a series of pirouettes and *tours en l'air*. There are no little *balancés* to give the dancer a breather, no preparations—like step, step, jump—to help him gain elevation. As Baryshnikov once wrote, it's up and down and up and down with no transitions, and therefore a killer on the legs.

It happens that this fabled variation was a last-minute substitute for a first version, which Youskevitch described as having small steps and a contemporary flavor. He didn't like it and asked Balanchine to change it. He wanted something "more in the grand manner," he said. One night when Balanchine was in the studio, he noticed Youskevitch practicing double *ronds de jambe en l'air*. Balanchine thought for a bit, then started a new solo beginning with those *ronds de jambe*. He finished the whole solo in about five minutes. Youskevitch thought it fit him like a glove.

It's not surprising that Balanchine could polish off the solo so quickly, because it's not really a piece of choreography. It's more like a classroom exercise, a brutally difficult one. The rest of *Theme* is indeed choreographed, although it does have by Balanchine's standards an unadorned use of classroom vocabulary that makes it closer to Petipa than any other Balanchine ballet I can think of.

Close but different. The pas de deux, especially, has signature Petipa moments in its courtly bows, extended promenades, and difficult balances on one foot for the ballerina. Yet these standard virtuoso moves are all absorbed into the music's lyric energy, so that one is hardly aware of the red flags of which the dancers are surely aware. All one sees and feels is a continuous flow of movement. There are also bits of modernization, particularly in the partnering. I think especially of the ballerina's little hops onto pointe in the beginning of the pas de deux, and the boosts she gets from her partner so that she can travel on the hops; and in the final movement, the way her partner slides her foot along the floor while she is in arabesque after he brings her down from a lift. Otherwise, everything we see has direct links to the Russian Imperial language and its close relationship to the classroom. This is probably why ballerinas and cavaliers often describe the choreography as "exposed." There's not even any special musical dynamic with which a ballerina can embroider her dancing, as there are in parts of *Tschaikovsky Piano Concerto No. 2* (Balanchine's preferred spelling of Tchaikovsky) or the Bizet *Symphony in C*, which Balanchine made just months before *Theme*. I suppose it's the very choreographic simplicity of *Theme* that makes it so daunting.

For me, the combination of the beauty of the dance step itself and the simple way it is shown reaches a peak in the short, slow section that the ballerina dances with eight other women. Supported by two of those dancers, she slowly unfolds her leg in a développé first in a *croisé* position, then *effacé*, then *écarté*. She then poses in a deep arabesque and concludes this reverie with an attitude to the back. All the while, the ensemble slowly curls inward and out, surrounding her like a garland. Never has this rather baldly stated primer on *épaulement* and the basic positions a dancer may strike been so sweetly grave, so full of pride. In some performances the ballerina seems to be showing us her most precious jewels. Then—boom!—it's over. Tchaikovsky hurtles into a brilliant allegro, and the ballerina follows suit with a dazzling cascade of turns and jumps.

New York City Ballet. Gelsey Kirkland. *Theme and Variations*. Choreography by George Balanchine © The George Balanchine Trust. Photo, Jerome Robbins Dance Division, The New York Public Library for the Performing Arts, Astor, Lenox and Tilden Foundations.

American Ballet Theatre. Ashley Tuttle. *Theme and Variations*. Choreography by George Balanchine © The George Balanchine Trust. Photo by © Costas.

The sequence with the ballerina and her eight attendants is foreshadowed in a section where the four demi-soloists do leg extensions in *effacé* (open) and *croisé* (crossed) positions, each supported by two women who revolve first one way, then the other. This contrast between open and crossed positions, which is a fundamental cornerstone of ballet's language, gets further play in the opening phrases of the ballet, when the principals do simple *pliés* and *tendus* in *croisé* and *effacé*. The phrase is then picked up by the ensemble and later by the man in his first solo.

The distinction between positions in which the dancer is completely open to the audience and those in which she faces us with the leg crossed forward or back so that her body is less exposed, more shadowed, accounts obviously for the geometric complexities with which the dancer occupies space. It's all these geometries that make ballet so compelling. Balanchine always plumbed these aspects of technique for their maximum possibilities, but in *Theme and Variations* he makes a big deal of it. For me, this attention he pays to *effacé* and *croisé* explains why *Theme* is as limpid as it is grand. It pays tribute to the inner stuffing of Petipa's choreography as much as to the tutu-and-tiara glamour of the grand manner.

Theme and Variations has always been a staple of American Ballet Theatre's repertory. The only Balanchine work in its repertory through the 1980s, it has been extremely useful as a filler of the "big classical ballet" slot. The New York City Ballet has never had a shortage of such ballets, but Balanchine did bring it into his own company in 1960, casting Violette Verdy and Edward Villella as the principals. In 1970, with Gelsey Kirkland and Villella as the leads, *Theme* became the fourth and final movement of a new ballet using the complete Suite No. 3. The newly created movements were not top-drawer—Balanchine was in a deep brood over the departure of Suzanne Farrell—and so *Theme and Variations* glistened ever more brightly.

The Nutcracker

My memory of children's birthday parties is that they ended in a heap of tears. There were several reasons for this: there was not enough food or there was too much, there were too many organized games or it was a free-for-all, the birthday girl got too many presents while the guests got none, there was not enough supervision by the adults or they hovered.

The Christmas party Balanchine staged for the first act of *The Nutcracker* gets it all right. There is idle time, where Balanchine deliberately sketched the action and pantomime in order to leave room for improvisation, and there are set social dances. In some of them children and adults dance together; in others the kids are on their own. Whenever there is the threat of disorder, the adults are there to the rescue. The Nutcracker doll, which impish Fritz breaks, is lovingly bandaged for Marie to cradle; and no one tells her to get over it. Although the party takes place in one room, there is ample breathing space for the parents to do what they want to do, which is to chat, and for the children to play. Here is a live-and-let-live world, although each group is true to its respective nature. The children scamper, and the parents stroll. Both groups observe Tchaikovsky's score, yet the children move allegro, the adults andante.

It's no wonder that many people prefer the first act to the second, even though the second is where most of the dancing is. One reason is that the divertissements in the Land of Sweets are a mixed bag. The Waltz of the Flowers is an incomparably sumptuous ensemble dance, but Hot Chocolate, Coffee, and Tea are hack work. The deliberately low-key Marzipan variation may have been intended as the "think" piece of the group, but nowadays one is mostly aware of its repetitiveness. The main reason, though,

New York City Ballet. Alexander Ritter as Drosselmeyer. *The Nutcracker.* Choreography by George Balanchine © The George Balanchine Trust. Photo by © Costas.

why Act I is the more exciting is that this is where the ballet's fantasy most profoundly unfolds. It's where Marie dreams of the growing Christmas tree. (When Balanchine was planning the ballet in 1953 there was concern about the amount of money he wanted for the tree and its journey upward. "But *The Nutcracker*," he replied, "*is* the tree.") It's in the first act that Marie saves the Nutcracker from being killed by the Mouse King. Then she magically glides through a snow forest on the very bed, now many times larger, on which she had lain her Nutcracker doll to rest. Gliding through a downy forest, guided by invisible forces, free to dream her dreams without fear of getting lost—did Balanchine know he was reading the fantasies of his audience, or didn't we know they are our fantasies until Balanchine showed them to us?

The conventional understanding of the story is that Marie has a dream that eventually takes her to the Land of Sweets. When the divertissements are over she wakes up in her house and rubs her eyes in wonderment. Here is Balanchine's understanding of the story, quoted in Nancy Reynolds's

Repertory in Review: "Actually, it's not a dream. It's the reality that Mother didn't believe. The story was written by Hoffmann against society. He said that society, the grown-ups, really have no imagination, that they try to suppress the imagination of children. . . . They didn't understand that nonreality is the real thing." Thus, in Balanchine's version of the ballet, the curtain comes down with Marie and the Prince flying through the air in a sleigh driven by reindeer. (In the earliest production, the City Center had no flying equipment, so the children sailed away in a walnut boat.) For all we know, they could still be sailing, or flying. It's good-bye home, good-bye Mom, and good-bye to all that.

Good-bye to Freud as well. In some productions, the dancers that Marie encounters in her dream are the people she knows in real life. No such alignment exists in Balanchine's version. Certain objects from her daily life undergo dreamlike transformation—toy soldiers, the curtains in her living room, her nutcracker doll, and so forth—but the people in her dream are pure fantasy. Why else dream, Balanchine might ask, if not to be somewhere else? In some productions Drosselmeyer gets a Freudian cast. He is not only odd, but erotically charged, speaking to the sexual impulses of the preadolescent heroine. In Balanchine's version it's enough that Drosselmeyer scare her by perching on top of a grandfather clock and making terrible faces.

There's an interesting paradox, though, in Balanchine's homage to non-reality. Although events are not fettered by reality, they must be plausible. The reindeer sleigh that Marie and her consort ride was Balanchine's idea. I was very struck by the importance and pride he gave this choice of animal. He chose reindeer, he said in Solomon Volkov's *Balanchine's Tchaikovsky*, because they really do drive sleighs. Many of his other ballets move into a dreamlike or imaginary world that becomes a Balanchinian reality. *Serenade* is the most spectacular example, but it's not an overstatement to say that all of his ballets begin where *Nutcracker* ends—in an eternal dream. The difference is that in the other ballets the dancers don't need to dream to be in a dream. The curtain rises, usually with a blue cyclorama as décor, and, presto!, you're there, in a timeless, placeless space. The dancers don't need a plot device to get them there; they don't need to lie down on a bed and fall asleep or take opium (like the hero in *La Bayadère*) or search for swans (like the Prince in *Swan Lake*). The accent on the plausible in *The*

Nutcracker is a concession to a logic that Balanchine felt unnecessary in his other ballets. As he said, " *The Nutcracker* is for children. They must be able to understand."

What if the children rode off on kangaroos instead of reindeer? The audience would find it "silly," Balanchine said. So, too, the sight of adults pretending to be children. In other productions in Russia, England, and the United States' Joffrey Ballet adult dancers take the role of children in the party scene. There are practical reasons for doing this. It takes much time to rehearse children, and if a company tours it doesn't have to round up a different cast of children for each city it visits. There are artistic reasons as well. Having an all-adult party allows for more complex dancing in the first act, and for many choreographers, especially Russians, more dancing equals a more modern approach to a nineteenth-century ballet. Pantomime is old-fashioned, Russians say. Having seen any number of productions in which adults play children, I can say that the effect is cloying and implausible.

Probably Balanchine would feel the same, but the main reason why he chose to use children is that the practice is a continuation of the Imperial system in which he grew up and which he continued to admire. Involving young students in the heart of theater life was a strategy employed by Petipa as much as by Bournonville in Denmark. It taught children discipline and might inspire them to pursue dancing as a career. It certainly did that for Balanchine, who had in mind to run away from dancing school until he appeared as a cherub in *The Sleeping Beauty*. Just standing on stage amid all the glory of that production hooked him. He also danced in the St. Petersburg *Nutcracker*, choreographed by Ivanov but, according to Balanchine, mapped out by Petipa. He played the Mouse King and the Prince, and as a professional dancer led the hoop dance (called Candy Canes in his own version). How much choreography and how many staging ideas he incorporated into his own *Nutcracker* is open to question, but he remembered enough about the original version to help Willam Christensen mount a production for the San Francisco Ballet in 1944, ten years before his own premiered.

That 1944 *Nutcracker* is the first complete version performed in the United States, but it was Balanchine's that became the national standard and the father of the hundreds of subsequent productions that now play across the nation. So ingrained has it become in family life that it's a measuring rod of a child's development. Friends will ask me with a tone revealing that only one answer will do, "Is my child old enough to see *The Nutcracker?*" The last time I saw it, a baby no more than six months old was sitting behind me. Her mother insisted that her baby loved it.

Coming from the opposite spectrum, as an old-timer, I still love it too. The white bed gliding through the white and green forest still fills me with awe and yearning. The mouse costumes designed by Karinska still delight. The soaring Christmas tree still sends spiritual surges through me as it makes concrete the ecstatic music of Tchaikovsky, which seems to me undanceable except by a tree. I have to say, though, that the journey of the tree in the very first years of performance, when I myself was one of the kids on stage, was more exciting than it is today. Back then, the machinery lifting the tree upward and the electrical wiring that gave it its twinkling lights were not up to snuff. As a soldier, I could get a peek at the dance of the tree. How it struggled to rise, how it quivered and heaved in its quest to soar! But often something went wrong with the electricity. The lights on the tree would blink on and off, and sometimes there was a smell—something burning? I vividly remember thinking as I stood in the soldiers' cupboard, waiting for the cue to charge the mice, Well, if you've got to die, this is the way to do it—going up in flames to this beautiful music.

A couple of other things have changed for the worse, too. When I was a child in the party scene, our movements about the stage were looser. Today, every gesture is set in stone. I miss some of the rough edges and spontaneity of the early years, although our relative freedom probably made for a messy-looking stage picture at times. The most substantial change is the structure of the grand pas de deux for the Sugar Plum Fairy and Cavalier. Originally, Balanchine adhered to the traditional Petipa form for the big number. The ballerina and *danseur noble* had full variations each, plus a pas de deux and coda. It was done in one block. Now the ballerina does her variation at the beginning of Act II, attended by little angels. The cavalier no longer has a complete variation, but gets to do a few jumps to music borrowed from the coda. Thus, what should be the dance climax of the entire ballet is chopped up and shortened. This is heresy!

New York City Ballet. Paloma Herrera in the Waltz of the Flowers. *The Nutcracker*. Choreography by George Balanchine © The George Balanchine Trust. Photo by © Costas.

Nevertheless, the essence of the Sugar Plum Fairy role remains intact. The choreography for the Dewdrop, in the Waltz of the Flowers, is thrilling, but she is not the ballerina of the ballet. The Sugar Plum, dressed in a classical tutu for her pas de deux (although not for her variation earlier on) and moving with measured grandeur and a formality reminiscent of the grand pas de deux in *The Sleeping Beauty*, is mistress of the land. If little Marie is thinking about whom she'd like to be when she grows up—although there is no reason to believe that her thoughts flow in that direction—the Sugar Plum would be just the right sort to emulate.

Western Symphony

1954

Western Symphony was Balanchine's first hit with an American theme. It has a glorious score by Hershy Kay, which sets western tunes in symphonic form. The other factor making the ballet an immediate success with the public was the idea behind the ballet, which juxtaposes familiar cowboy tunes with classical dancing. The sight of the New York City Ballet dancing to "Red River Valley" as though it were Mozart was irresistible. By the time the curtain comes down on the entire cast pirouetting like mad to "Hail, hail, the gang's all here," Balanchine has you in the thrall of his joke, and of his serious proposition as well, that ballet is versatile and durable.

This particular brand of American ballet was Balanchine's invention and is pretty clear cut: you take the basic classical technique and garnish it with attitudes and gestures suggested by the music. The general concept of an "American ballet" is murky in definition, however. Does it mean ballet with an American story, or does it describe a style of dancing? The confusion about the term persists today, but suffice it to say that the notion of a ballet that is American rather than Russian preoccupied the Balanchine enterprise from the very start. Rather, it preoccupied Kirstein, who brought Balanchine to America in 1933. In his many polemical articles in the 1930s he called for a national ballet whose dancers would be trained in classical technique in America and whose music and subject matter would be American. Accordingly, in 1935 Balanchine created *Alma Mater*, with music by Kay Swift. It took place during a football game at Yale, and the villain wore a coonskin coat. When queried about his knowledge of football, Balanchine's response, quoted in *Repertory in Review*, was, "Once they took

me to see football, and, of course, I had been to soccer in England. It's practically the same thing—well, that is, there's a ball and they're running."

Alma Mater might have been good fun, but we don't know because it
didn't survive. In any case, it was Kirstein who then took up the cause of an
American ballet. In 1936 he founded Ballet Caravan, without Balanchine's
participation, and during the next four years produced eight ballets on
American subjects, including *Pocahontas*, *Filling Station*, and *Billy the Kid*.
Meanwhile, Balanchine made dances on Broadway and in Hollywood.

The idea of an American ballet didn't surface again for Balanchine until
1950, when he and Jerome Robbins made *Jones Beach* for the New York
City Ballet. The dancers wore swimsuits, and the last movement was called
"Hot Dogs." This work didn't last long either, although not necessarily
because of its subject matter or the way it was treated. As described by
Robbins, the choreographic process spelled failure. Balanchine would choreograph a couple of minutes of a section, then Robbins would take over
and do a few more minutes until turning over the reins to Balanchine for a
few minutes more. "The dancers didn't know *what* was going on!" Robbins
said. Perhaps the choreographers didn't either.

It's clear that making ballets about hot dogs and football games and
iconic American figures was not Balanchine's cup of tea. Yet in the early
1950s, when the City Ballet was trying to find a large public, there was a
need to come up with a populist angle. I don't know if Balanchine liked hot
dogs and sports, but he did love Westerns. A ballet with a western theme
and music engaged him personally and so was a viable possibility. As for the
idea of mounting a classical ballet to such a setting . . . let's just chalk it up
to his imagination and, if I may add, to his profound belief in basic ballet
language. Using that language, Balanchine believed that he'd end up on his
feet. He was right. One could argue that *Western Symphony* is no different
from the second act of *The Nutcracker*. This is right, too, in essence, but
perhaps a bit hidebound. The difference between composers *does* affect the
feel of a ballet.

Western Symphony is in three movements. (The fourth, a scherzo, was
dropped about five years after the 1954 premiere.) True to the conventions
of symphonies, the first movement is the most extended, musically and
choreographically. Wedged within allegro portions is a full pas de deux
for the principal couple, plus solos for each. The fact that the pas de deux

is danced to honky-tonk piano does not erase its formality; the ballerina even does a *grand développé à la seconde* when the music reaches its grandest scale—a favorite step of Balanchine's to mark the acme of a duet. We know we're out West because the men in the ensemble saunter and swagger and tip their cowboy hats, while the ladies saucily thrust their fannies out when they're at rest. These embellishments are all Balanchine needs to establish a tone in alignment with the music. One other factor: no matter which company is performing *Western*, the dancers always look happy and snappy as the Western tunes course through their bodies. One can't underestimate the importance of Hershy Kay's score to the success of the ballet.

The adagio section features one fairly dopey cowboy who dreams of romance—or is it cows?—as he strums his guitar; four small horses who sweetly follow his tugs at the reins; and one ballerina, whose entrance the horses duly acknowledge with curtsies when she first passes by. The section is a humorous rendition of the boy-meets-girl, boy-loses-girl scenario of many romantic ballets. The ballerina's farewell to the cowboy is a sendup of *Swan Lake*, and there are other allusions to romantic gestures and situations as well. Conventions of the pas de deux also get a ribbing. Sometimes

New York City Ballet. *Western Symphony*. Choreography by George Balanchine © The George Balanchine Trust. Photo by © Costas.

Balanchine inserts deliberate awkwardness into the partnering, as when the woman swoons backward in her cowboy's arms and then is placed face down, her nose almost touching the floor. (That face-down position was once a movement in *Concerto Barocco*, but Balanchine removed it and saved it for a sunnier day.)

"The dance with the hat" was critic P. W. Manchester's immediate nickname for the last, Rondo, section, because the ballerina sports a *belle époque* chapeau designed by Barbara Karinska. It's made of thin black horsehair and a feather or two, which Karinska manipulated into a delicate confection of curlicue lines that soared upward on one side. The hat was a marvelous construction in itself, but it was Tanaquil Le Clercq who justified the Rondo's nickname. She endowed the hat with some of her own qualities as a dancer—elegance and wit. She turned that upward tilt of the hat into something positively rakish. A half-century later, I still see Le Clercq's long, tapered legs speaking to the curlicued hat in mischievous conversation.

Balanchine loved send-'em-home-happy finales, and he found a different way to choreograph each one. The finale in *Western* begins when the entire cast jigs in unison in six straight lines. The novel bit is when the outer lines suddenly jig into the center of the stage and back again as the music changes chords. The stage looks like shifting panels, and the effect is seismic for reasons I still can't figure out. Perhaps it has to do with the strong horizontal surges meeting a surge in the music. Maybe. But what's certain is that these shifting lines topped off with pirouettes en masse sends you home smiling.

Western Symphony's closest relative is *Stars and Stripes* (1957), in which drum majorettes dance all the steps they learned in ballet school to the music of Sousa. Other works falling under the rubric of "American ballet" are *Square Dance*, *Who Cares?*, and *Native Dancers*. These ballets portray an upbeat America. A mere week after the premiere of *Western Symphony* Balanchine presented the flip side of America, *Ivesiana*, to various pieces by Charles Ives. This America is bleak, brutal, and confounding and was obviously not as popular as the happy pieces. None of them, of course, fulfills the ideals that Kirstein had in mind when he brought Balanchine to America. *Ivesiana* is just too strange and impenetrable. About alienation, it tends to alienate the audience as well. The happy ballets are not what I would call deeply American. They are pastiches. There are no adjust-

New York City Ballet. Tanaquil Le Clercq. *Western Symphony*. Choreography by George Balanchine © The George Balanchine Trust. Photo, Jerome Robbins Dance Division, The New York Public Library for the Performing Arts, Astor, Lenox and Tilden Foundations.

ments in the dancers' technique, no insertions of vernacular gesture to illustrate an American theme. It's *glissade, assemblé, passé,* pirouette all the way. Balanchine's pervasive use of classical technique—with a few exceptions, among them *Ivesiana*—precludes a truly American dance style.

Many observers have cited the dancers' speed and energy as specifically American. It's true that Balanchine dancers and urban Americans move quickly, but what is paramount in his allegro is intricate, delicate footwork, and I'm not sure that these ultra-refined qualities are typically American. The energy factor is a better candidate for Americanness, "energy" meaning giving every step its full measure and extending one's line to the utmost— in other words, giving one's all. Balanchine didn't use the word "energy" in class. He used to say, "Look alive!" If total commitment to the moment, every moment, is American, then perhaps it is fair to say that he did instill in his dancers an American style. But I've heard total definition of every single moment in the concert hall as well. Would one then say that Glenn Gould, for example, played the piano with an American style? This heightened definition is a way of making art. In ballet, it was the Balanchine way. To call it an American way is journalistic puffery.

The irony in these thoughts is that the one uniquely American thing to which Balanchine was drawn does not crop up in the American ballets— jazz. You see it in the pelvis when it thrusts forward, in the wide swing of the hips, and most of all in the syncopated dialogues between dance and music. The jazz is in *Concerto Barocco, The Four Temperaments,* and the Stravinsky ballets.

Square Dance

1957

Square Dance is an American ballet with a couple of differences. The music is not by an American, but by Vivaldi and Corelli. In other works of this type, Balanchine approaches the music—western tunes, Sousa, Gershwin, Ives—at face value and with complete respect. In *Square Dance* he comments on the music. Some critics believe that the connection between these two Baroque masters and square dancing is that the music is based on old dance forms. My intuition tells me that Balanchine imagined a square-dance setting because the music is jolly and simple. Set for string orchestra, it's what you'd call fiddle, rather than violin, music. At the time of *Square Dance*'s premiere, in November 1957, Vivaldi and Corelli were enjoying a huge revival in the concert hall. Perhaps, Balanchine countered, they belonged in the barn rather than the concert hall.

In the first version—for there are two—the fiddlers sat on one side of the stage while the dancers went about their business on the other side, giving the whole picture a cozy, if somewhat cramped, atmosphere. The men wore red bandannas. What clinched the square-dance conceit was the participation of a caller, Elisha Keeler, who belted out doggerel verse while the fiddlers fiddled away like mad. "Here come Nick and Pat," Keeler sang out with a twang, "watch them go wickety-whack."

Nick and Pat were easy to figure out; they were Nicholas Magallanes and Patricia Wilde, the leads. In the 1950s the public at the New York City Center, where the City Ballet was in residence, was still small but avid for the next Balanchine installment, whatever it would be. One never knew where he would take us. In 1951 he presented—*mon dieu*!—the second act of *Swan Lake*. A few years later *The Nutcracker* and *Opus 34* (a nightmarish probe into Schoenberg's music) bowed hand in hand. Ten days after *Square Dance*'s premiere came *Agon*. The public was loyal and felt intimate with the company and its dancers as it hitched a seat on the joy ride. So it was not at all presumptuous to call Magallanes and Wilde by their nicknames; nor did it impose a familiarity that wasn't already there. And, of course, it was in keeping with the populist spirit of the ballet.

But "wickety-whack"? What was that? It didn't matter once you got the hang of the ballet's conceit; it didn't matter that *Square Dance* makes no reference to square dancing. For one thing, the cast is six couples plus a lead couple. Clearly, Balanchine had no intention of making good on the title he chose. The concept was a gimmick and a little joke, perhaps, especially if one takes, as I do, the pairing of the music and square dancing as commentary on the music. One cannot imagine Balanchine dreaming up the caller bit to Bach.

Balanchine once said, "You always have to be serious, even about your jokes—especially about your jokes." The actual dancing in *Square Dance* is serious. It is one of the most intense and extended explorations into *petit allegro* technique that Balanchine ever made. (A contender would be *Ballo della Regina*, made some twenty years after *Square Dance*'s premiere.) Because the pace is so quick, the dancers must hug the floor in all kinds of leg beats and tiny jumps (like *emboîtés*). The supported jumps dart up and down; they don't soar. The emphasis is on speed rather than rhythm, although Balanchine occasionally tosses into the mix a catchy dynamic. I think especially of the first movement's prime motif—three *emboîtés*, a pause with one leg suspended in the air, then an *entrechat*. That pause is music to one's eyes, because it inserts into the music's four-square beat a delightful cranny, making it richer. The trick is for the dancers to make the intricate weave legible to the audience, and joyous.

When I write "dancers," I refer to the ensemble as well as the lead couple. Normally, the leads' choreography is a good deal more difficult than the ensemble's, but in this ballet there is parity (almost), a point Balanchine emphasizes in passages where the ensemble and leads play follow the leader. Although *Square Dance* is modest in scale, it was a leap forward in terms of the demands Balanchine made on the corps de ballet.

For contrast, there is a short adagio for the lead couple at the beginning of the second movement. Given the friendly demeanor of the ballet, it is curiously formal, beginning with a long introduction whose courtly manners recall the grand pas de deux of Russian classics. He bows to her, she bows to him, he offers his hand, she accepts it with flourish (that is, with highly articulated wrists and fingers), and so forth. The dance proper brings to mind the elegance, simplicity, and long singing line of the pas de deux in *Concerto Barocco*. The ballerina—for the leading lady does become a ballerina in this section—must find a way to keep the pulse going and going despite the simplicity of her movements and the many repetitions of certain phrases. (One of them the couple repeats five times!) The task of keeping it all alive is as much a challenge as the allegro parts.

In 1957 Balanchine had in Patricia Wilde a dancer who excelled in allegro and was very good in adagio, too (although it took a while for him to give her the role of Odette). *Square Dance* was, I think, her crowning achievement. Her memory of *Square Dance*'s germination is especially happy. In the 1950s Balanchine and his wife, Tanaquil Le Clercq, had a country house in Connecticut, and Wilde, her husband, and sometimes other friends would visit the Balanchines for weekends of gardening, cooking, working on home-improvement projects. In the fall of 1957 Keeler would join the group and regale everyone with the rhymes he was inventing for the ballet. Balanchine's only request was that he avoid French terminology. Wilde's only worry was how to find the stamina to sustain herself. Balanchine's advice was to dance the ballet three times in a row. This Wilde did, and it worked. But, she said in later years, how she would have loved it had the long male solo existed in the original version, for it would have given her a rest.

In 1976 Balanchine rethought *Square Dance* and made a vastly different sequel. Given that the choreography remained more or less the same, it is remarkable how dissimilar the two versions are. He eliminated the caller and placed the orchestra in the pit. He also created a new, somber solo for the man. Presto: a new *Square Dance* so independent of a concept, any concept, as to make the ballet's title meaningless.

In truth, the role of the caller—perhaps it is more fair to say, the style of Keeler's delivery—had grown problematical. Taking his cue from the music, he was unstoppable! Another caller from a Joffrey Ballet production years later took a more relaxed approach, to the benefit of all. Soon after the premiere of the first *Square Dance* Kirstein had wanted to ditch the caller, but Balanchine objected, saying that without the square-dance idea the ballet would be like an inferior *Barocco*. This is an exaggeration, I think, but there is a grain of truth to it. In any case, by 1976 the Americanization of the repertory was no longer necessary. The public did not have to be convinced that ballet was as integral to American culture as any other art form.

The change that most affected the ballet's tone was placing the musicians in the pit. By enlarging the dancing space to the full stage, *Square Dance* was more formal, pristine, "serious," if you will. The larger the stage, the more weight a dance has; it's as if dancers expand their range and presence to fill the larger dimensions.

The solo, for Bart Cook, also added gravitas. Set to a Corelli sarabande, it is a long, slow meditation full of statuesque poses and courtly gesture sprinkled with lunges and backbends. Cook had an unusually supple and expressive back, which is perhaps what prompted Balanchine to set this solo on him and which might have prompted him to make the solo in the first place. This dance for the beautiful back harkens to the Melancholic section of *The Four Temperaments* and, in its closing passages, back even

New York City Ballet. Merrill Ashley and Sean Lavery. *Square Dance*. Choreography by George Balanchine © The George Balanchine Trust. Photo by © Costas.

New York City Ballet. Bart Cook. *Square Dance*. Choreography by George Balanchine © The George Balanchine Trust. Photo by © Costas.

farther to *Apollo*, when the sarabande dancer lunges forward toward the audience and then bends deeply from side to side. That frontal assault is astonishing and gives the whole ballet a dark coloration that is as far from square dancing as a waltz.

The addition of the male solo also made *Square Dance* less of a women's ballet. There is another reason, though, for the new parity between the sexes. Paradoxically, as the dancing space expanded, the dance style of the female contingent contracted. Balanchine cast Kay Mazzo in Wilde's role, and the ballerina part thereby became less robust and virtuoso, more dainty and charming. With Wilde, *Square Dance* really was a hoedown. Any number of women who succeeded Mazzo in the part have stronger allegro technique, especially in *batterie*, but interestingly the more polite version of the ballet has become the tradition at the City Ballet.

Agon

1957

By consensus, *Agon* is one of Balanchine's masterpieces; many would claim it to be *the* masterpiece. The only points of dispute are: how do you say it, and what does it mean? Is it agon with a long *a*, or agon as in agony? Some people Frenchify it, as ahgohn, while those with knowledge of Greek, from which the word is derived, pronounce it ahgoon. Is the accent on the first or last syllable? As for the word's meaning, Greek experts hold that there is no really adequate translation. The majority opinion understands the word to mean "contest" or "struggle," the only problem being that Balanchine's *Agon* is not about contests or struggles.

Moving laterally from notions of struggle and contest, however, one arrives at the idea of tension, and that word is a very fine description of the ballet. It is not that *Agon* is literally about tension. Rather, the experience of watching it produces tension in the viewer, and within the ballet itself are many oppositional forces, or artistic tensions. Most of Balanchine's ballets indicate no desire to represent their time; indeed, with their projections of romantic love in some cases and cheerfulness in others, and of graciousness and glamour all the time, his work can be seen as a refutation of the manners and morals of the twentieth century. *Agon* is the exception. It was premiered by the City Ballet on December 1, 1957, with a commissioned score by Stravinsky, and because it so brims with tension it truly does embody the age in which it was created.

The most characteristic fact about *Agon* is that there are at least two actions happening at the same time, and the effort to absorb these multiple actions produces a tension that starts in the eye and works its way into one's muscles. Balanchine achieves this multiplicity of movement by adapting the musical canon structure to dance, wherein a step or a few steps are repeated by the dancers on consecutive beats, creating a polyphonic effect. This device is a favorite of Balanchine's, but one difference between the canons in *Agon* and those in other ballets is that in *Agon* canons are in almost constant play. You can count the number of passages in which everyone is doing the same thing at the same time. A moment like the beginning of the last section, when four couples are evenly spread in a line across the front of the stage, all doing supported *développés*, is like an oasis of calm, when one walks in the street at dawn. But soon four more women enter, bringing the cast to its grand total of twelve, and it's off to the races again: twelve people dancing on twelve different beats. Now if those dancers were doing twelve different steps in canon, the effect would approach chaos. One would tune out, back off; the mind would wander. It is the very fact that the same phrases are repeated *not quite* in unison, but within the blink of an eye, that the audience stays in the game. We perceive the order and the strategy; we just have to be alert, very alert, to take it all in.

When two people are dancing in canon, the effect is often witty. I think of the duet for two men (the "bransle simple"), who move in such close proximity that they seem like two puppies yapping at each other's heels. When Balanchine sets the entire cast in canon, the effect is of a small, well-oiled machine, again witty for its compact contours. Perhaps these are the moments Balanchine had in mind when he called *Agon* "a computer that smiles." Today, he might specify a laptop computer, so compressed is *Agon*'s spatial design. The dancers in *Agon* cover little space, which would be surprising in any ballet but is all the more so in a ballet remarkable for its forceful impact. The *Agon* group lives on a tight little island, and there is no better measure of this than when the dancers cut loose—when Balanchine divides his cast into groups of three or four and sends them in canon across the *entire* stage. The effect is galvanic, exhilarating. Yeah baby, go! But watch out for the intersections (which they do).

The ballet has many such perilous paths and safe landings; Balanchine even goes so far as to punctuate some of those landings with a touch of flourish—amusingly exaggerated bows and *ports de bras* reminiscent of Renaissance court dances (from which Stravinsky took his inspiration). My own favorite safe landing is the end of the second pas de trois, when the woman is caught in midair.

New York City Ballet. Peter Martins and Suzanne Farrell. *Agon.* Choreography by George Balanchine © The George Balanchine Trust. Photo by © Costas.

Ironically, the most famous section of *Agon*, the pas de deux, is the one part where tension and wit are not intertwined. Not accidentally, the two dancers are not engaged in canonic dialogue. The tension inherent in their dancing does not involve the intricacies of timing but rather the exploratory investigations of bodily shapes and methods of partnering. And also skin color, at least at the beginning of the ballet's history.

Arthur Mitchell, who danced this duet with Diana Adams, is black. When the ballet premiered in 1957, the sight of black and white skins dancing together with such intimacy was new, not to mention visually stunning. Although no fuss was made about the racial aspect of the pas de deux, Mitchell has said that Balanchine was well aware of the black-and-white contrast and used it to contribute to the electric energy of the section. Another tension-making aspect was that the audience had never seen a ballerina in such extreme acrobatic positions (*Prodigal Son* may be the exception), nor had we seen a man support her while lying flat on his back. Their duet was literally new territory for the audience. Whether or not it was still new territory for the dancers by the time of the premiere, Adams and Mitchell nonetheless created the illusion of dancing on a new frontier at the moment of performance. This illusion was enhanced by Adams's naturally tense disposition. Although a dancer of poignant lyricism and vulnerability, she had a nervous edge about her, and it found a perfect foil in the *Agon* pas de deux. Your heart pounded for her, and those slight tremblings of the dancers' enjoined hands seemed much less the conceit than it does today. In the 1950s, you had better believe that those hands were shaking!

Today, of course, *Agon* is in the dance culture. The duet dancers must pretend that they are going where they have never been before, but if the performance is good the ruse works. Yet tension is still there right in the bones of the choreography, involving the emotional relationship between the dancers. With an almost Tolstoyan nuance, the duet embodies the volatile climate in which an intimate couple lives. The duet is in constant flux between moments of tenderness and aggression, assertiveness and submission, challenge and compliance, escape and return. The whole thing trembles with change, and the same moments change coloration from performance to performance. The moment when the woman, held aloft, spreads her legs into a split can look like a women's-lib banner replete with defiance, or a yearning for freedom, or a flower about to bloom. In other such acrobatic moments the man can seem to be forcing the woman into impossible positions, or tenderly guiding her into positions he foresees will be beautiful. And in the final gesture, in which the woman bends over the kneeling man, one can read either her offer of safety to him—striking a maternal note—or simple exhaustion. In the first years of performance, that final gesture was muted, making the audience unsure about whether or not it was the right time to applaud. These days it is emphatic, signaling The End. Confusion about when a section is over is a kind of tension that Balanchine did not have in mind.

Indeed, for all the emotional ambiguities of the pas de deux and the canonic complexities of the rest, *Agon* is as lucid and in control of itself as any ballet Balanchine ever created. This oppositional pull between clarity and complexity accounts, obviously, for yet another source of tension. And still another is in the play between quotidian moves and classical ones. At the quotidian end of the spectrum, as in the opening male quartet, is a cluster of lunges, pivots, kicks and walks—barely a *pas* in sight, let alone a virtuoso one. When the foremost virtuoso of his day, Baryshnikov, was dancing with American Ballet Theatre, a City Ballet dancer teasingly asked Balanchine why he didn't invite Baryshnikov into the City Ballet. Thinking of all those ordinary moves in *Agon*, Balanchine replied, "But what would he do here—this?"—and then pivoted his toe back and forth on the floor.

At the other, classical end of the spectrum is the duet for two women, the gailliard. All it is, more or less, is some *échappés*, *piqués*, and lots of *passés*—pure Petipa in its simplicity and purity of language. And as for the *passé*, this basic position of the leg is as much a motif of the ballet as the pivots and lunges. Of course, the angular line of the leg in *passé* as it breaks at the knee fits in nicely with the contemporary look of the ballet, but how typical of Balanchine's method to use so prominently a first-grader's step to serve his most advanced work.

By now it is a truism to say of Balanchine's genius that he moved forward by looking backward. But this double vision was forsaken in certain later ballets set to Stravinsky—namely the *Stravinsky Violin Concerto*, *Symphony in Three Movements*, and *Duo Concertant* of the 1972 Stravinsky Festival. In these later works, his interest in having the steps visually describe rhythms supersedes his interest in what the steps actually look like. In fact, Balanchine pretty much discards classical *pas*. If it weren't for the choreography's rhythmic vitality (and in some instances programmatic content), there wouldn't be much to look at. This is why this trio of ballets, however celebrated, is less masterly than *Agon*. *Agon* is the one where the pull between the nineteenth and twentieth centuries is most taut, where he looked in both directions with unparalleled force and boldness.

One can claim the same achievement for Stravinsky' score. It is based on a French Baroque dance manual by de Lauze, with accompanying music by Mersenne (hence the names assigned to the dances—gailliard, sarabande, bransle, etc.). Baroque-isms abound in the music, especially in its instrumentation. Yet *Agon* was one of Stravinsky's earliest forays into serial, or twelve-tone, technique. Stravinsky and Balanchine agreed that it is difficult music, to listen to and to play. There is a charming story, recorded in Bernard Taper's biography of Balanchine, about one of the rehearsals that Stravinsky attended in the fall of 1957. The rehearsal pianist complained that he didn't understand the music. "That's okay," Stravinsky replied, "I don't either."

Stravinsky's participation in rehearsals at the School of American Ballet's studios on Broadway in New York was the final phase of collaboration between the two men. Balanchine and Kirstein commissioned the score in 1953 or 1954 with funds from the Rockefeller Foundation. Stravinsky did not finish the score until April 1957, but in the interim, composer and choreographer spent a good deal of time working out the scenario. Stravinsky was a stickler for length, often saying that he couldn't begin to work until he knew exactly what length he was dealing with—down to the second. So he and Balanchine worked out the length of each section of the proposed ballet—down to the second.

Just as crucial to the ballet's structure, and ultimate elegance, it turns out, was their choice of the number of dancers. They chose twelve, the number choreographer Lar Lubovitch once called "the magic number," because it can be divided into quartets and trios. For the most dazzling exposition of "twelveness," one looks to *Agon*.

The ballet is in three parts, each divided into subparts. Tellingly, each of those subparts is described in the program, as it was in the original scenario, by the number of dancers. Thus part 1 breaks down into a pas de

Pacific Northwest Ballet. *Agon.* Choreography by George Balanchine © The George Balanchine Trust. Photo by © Costas.

quatre, double pas de quatre, and triple pas de quatre. The first subsection of part 2 is divided into two sets of pas de trois, which are actually six discrete dances for one, two, and three people. In this section, gender comes into play: two men versus one woman, and vice versa. Then comes the pas de deux. Part 3 is arranged as four duos, four trios, and then a male quartet. Whereupon *Agon* ends up where it began, down to the same step, with the four men turning toward the back of the stage one beat after the music has stopped. A zinger, that bit of timing!

It was Stravinsky's idea, by the way, to have the men face backward at the end, and he made one or two other choreographic suggestions as well. But what mostly occupied him at rehearsals were tempi. As a student at the School of American Ballet at the time, I had the marvelous fortune to sit in on two of those rehearsals. At one of them, I well remember, Stravinsky and Balanchine spent more time adjusting a metronome than anything else. And at the other one, Stravinsky watched the ballet's mathematical delicacy unfold with a smile on his face.

A series of photographs made during those rehearsals gives a good idea of the creators' high spirits. Stravinsky's face often bursts into a grin, as though he's just heard or told a terrific joke. Rarely a grinner or even a smiler, Balanchine's eyes are nevertheless animated with delight, as though he were thinking of a joke he might tell (or yet another subdivision of twelve to try out). His face looks noticeably haggard, however; indeed, he looks older in 1957 than he did twenty years later.

A year earlier, his wife, Le Clercq, had contracted polio in Denmark, while the City Ballet was on tour. It was a harrowing time for all; indeed, there were fears that Balanchine would never come back to New York. He and his paralyzed wife did eventually return to the United States in March 1957, but Balanchine went to Georgia to be with Le Clercq, where she was recuperating. Ballet was far from his mind. By the summer, however, back at his country house in Connecticut, he wrote a letter to Kirstein saying that a piano reduction of the *Agon* score had arrived and that the music was even more appetizing than his roses.

Against this background of tragedy came an extraordinarily intense period of work in the fall. *Agon* was hardly the only ballet in preparation. Balanchine was also creating *Square Dance*, which premiered a week before the Stravinsky. In the following January *Gounod Symphony* and *Stars and*

Stripes arrived. Except for the Gounod ballet, all are staples of the international repertory.

The year 1957 has become a legendary period in Balanchine's career, not only because of his prolificacy, but also because it was the most dramatic comeback he had made. Then as now, *Agon* was understood to be in a class by itself. (In its premiere season the City Ballet had to tack on a few performances to the programs because of ticket demand.) Yet it adds a beguiling aspect to *Agon*'s singularity to imagine Balanchine running back and forth among Stravinsky and Sousa and Gounod and the Vivaldi-cum-caller's twang. Was this outpouring of work a volcanic release from sorrow? Did it constitute in Balanchine's life at that time an inner agon, a contest in which he was the only player? Or a struggle against death?

To me, the truest illustration of the meaning of the word *agon* is a memory from 1957 of Melissa Hayden, cast as the single woman in the second pas de trois, working on a particular step from *Agon* in a corner of the studio during class. The step involves the front foot stepping crosswise and backward onto pointe in an arabesque and then quickly falling onto a flat foot. It is a signature movement for the men, but the women must grapple with it as well. Hayden repeated that step over and over for a period of days, first doing it slowly and then working up to tempo and gradually increasing the length of the step backward. Her face was intense and tense as she worked to achieve the required amplitude and speed of the maneuver. When she got it right, a slight smile would play around her mouth, but even the tense moments were buoyant—happy, one might say—in their focus and implied possibility of perfection.

On a really, really good night in the theater, *Agon* has that buoyancy, a lightheadedness that comes from purposeful work.

Donizetti Variations

1960

Artistic directors frequently say that opening ballets are hard to come by. With a smile they say that an opener is not easy to describe but that they know one when they see one. Openers tend to be pure expositions of dance style, concise in length (between fifteen and thirty minutes), set to pleasing music, and with a happy mood. Always the menu planner, Balanchine made many first courses. *Donizetti Variations* is one of them, along with *Ballo della Regina* (Verdi), *Allegro Brillante* (Tchaikovsky), *Concerto Barocco* (Bach), *Le Tombeau de Couperin* (Ravel), *Square Dance* (Vivaldi and Corelli), and *Raymonda Variations* (Glazounov), although the last mentioned might be too large in scale to fully qualify as a proper opener.

Donizetti Variations is not so large as it is never-ending. About twenty-five minutes long, it is divided into thirteen sections, which is more than twice the number of a typical ballet. Talk about a string of divertissements! *Donizetti* takes the proverbial out of the phrase and makes it literal. As a result of its "stringness," it's a difficult work to track in one's mind. Concepts like beginning, middle, and end or prologue, climax, and denouement don't reveal themselves as the ballet progresses. Although it is continuously sustained by bubbly spirits and charming dancing, it is somewhat shapeless. In hopes of finding a hidden shape, I sat down one day with a videotape and catalogued the sequence of sections with a note or two about how many dancers are in each one and what they're doing. The best summary I could come up with was "a string of divertissements."

The ballet is set to the ballet music from Act II of Donizetti's *Don Sebastian*. In its first year of life, in 1960, *Donizetti Variations* was called *Variations from Don Sebastian*. The change in title was wise, because only opera fans would recognize the name *Don Sebastian*. The opera was not the great success that Donizetti hoped for and has never entered the general opera repertory.

The ballet music has many delightful rhythms and melodies—in fact, it fully qualifies as *musique dansante*, the term Balanchine used to describe music that is especially suitable for choreography. However, each section of the score ends with the fanfare of a finale. Pretty soon one catches on that music signaling the end doesn't mean that it *is* the end; nevertheless, once the duet and solos for the principal couple have passed, you can't help but anticipate the ballet's conclusion with each succeeding section. Obviously, *Donizetti*'s string of finales reinforces the never-ending feel of the ballet.

It's natural to wonder why Balanchine chose this music and whether he had a notion of satirizing its bombast. The ballet does indeed have one satiric episode, but otherwise Balanchine shoots straight from the hip. The jokey moment follows the cluster of brilliant solos and coda for the male and female principals. The ensemble dancers, accompanied by music suggesting a crisis or storm, rush on and freeze into a melodramatic pose, their faces buried in the crook of their arms. One lady sees an opportunity to grab stage center and entertains us with a little solo of her own. She ends up stubbing her toe and hobbles back to her place within the group. (In an earlier, and I think funnier, version of the joke, a woman surveyed the histrionic postures, shrugged her shoulders incredulously, and trundled back to her spot.) Whereupon an adagio for everyone proceeds as if no joke had been made.

Apart from this bit, Balanchine makes no winking comments on the music. So one must assume that he liked it, because, as the ballet proves over and over, it gave him a platform for the virtuoso allegro dancing he so loved. The principal man's choreography is especially interesting because of its Bournonville-like quality. The man has many small beats and turns, so tightly sequenced that they allow no time for preparations. This quick up-and-down momentum is one reason why the ballet, like Bournonville's ballets, is often called "bubbly."

Bubbles and charm go hand in hand. One source of that charm is the particular way in which Balanchine uses the canon device. More often than not, his canons are hard to catch because the sequences of steps are fast and similar. *Agon* is a prime example. In *Donizetti* he chooses some

New York City Ballet. Helgi Tomasson. *Donizetti Variations*. Choreography by George Balanchine © The George Balanchine Trust. Photo by © Costas.

of the plunkity-plunk passages of music to "canonize," so that the whole business is laid out neatly and crisply. These canons are performed by three dancers, and one can easily follow the first step as it travels down the line while keeping track of the second and third steps as well. These canons for dummies are irresistible for their playful simplicity, and to my mind they constitute signature moments of the ballet.

The three-dancer makeup is the main grouping of the entire ballet. It is cast for six women and three men, plus the lead couple. It begins with each of the men escorting two women around the stage in a stately parade of arabesques. This is the only stately moment in *Donizetti*, while the pas de trois setup is a constant. Almost a constant—and here is where the craft enters. Balanchine opts for fluidity and variety rather than consistency. Thus, in some sections he reconfigures the nine-dancer ensemble (and its breakdown into three trios) into different schemes. In one part we have three couples dancing while three women stand on the side as onlookers. Another segment is a dance for four women, and as a measure of the "threesomeness" of the ballet, the quartet takes one up short. In case you haven't thought about it, and you probably haven't, there's a difference between a trio and a quartet. The first is chummy; the second is more neutral. *Donizetti* tells you about such things.

The most extended number-play occurs in the adagio for the ensemble. It begins with one active couple. Gradually (that is, gradually for this ballet) everyone is included in the dancing except for one woman. This discordant note is resolved when the nine people are redistributed in a new way—as two couples plus a grouping of four ladies and a man. Finally, the group resumes its three by three shape. And then it's on to the next section.

I love these playing-the-numbers moments for the same reasons I love Balanchine's play with body shapes, vocabulary, and patterns. It all reveals his mastery of form, his inventiveness, his wisdom in understanding that theatrical vitality can spring from rudimentary procedures. Once in a while the numbers game achieves metaphoric resonance. The most profound instance is in the andante of the Mozart *Divertimento No. 15*, premiered four years prior to the Donizetti piece. Working with an asymmetrical group of five ballerinas and three cavaliers, he interweaves the dancers so that there

New York City Ballet. *Left to right:* Todd Williams, Russell Kaiser, Arch Higgins. *Donizetti Variations.* Choreography by George Balanchine © The George Balanchine Trust. Photo by © Costas.

is never a wallflower. Aided by Mozart's sublime music, the passage comes to express social harmony and spiritual grace. *Donizetti* climbs to no such heights. The reshuffling of its groupings is just fun. Yet I find it interesting that Balanchine wanted to apply his Mozartian idea to another ballet as soon as possible, even if the music was by Donizetti.

A Midsummer Night's Dream

1962

Firefly season is in full swing as I write. In Central Park laughing children and their parents charge the beetles with glass jars and promises to release them from their captivity the next morning. Older folk sit on park benches and simply enjoy the spectacle. Everyone loves fireflies, including, apparently, George Balanchine, who as a child played an insect in a theatrical production of *A Midsummer Night's Dream*. For he begins his dance version of the play with a swarm of child insects and adult butterflies darting around the stage like fireflies. This being a ballet, however, the first bug to make an appearance is poised for flight appropriately in *tendu*.

Mendelssohn's music indicates the scurrying of nature's most fleet-footed creatures, but dancing insects aren't the only option for a choreographer. Ashton's *The Dream*, created in 1964, two years after the Balanchine version, sets dancing fairies to the same music and to marvelous effect. That Balanchine chose an insect corps de ballet tells one much about a central theme of *Midsummer*. It is an affectionate contemplation of nature in summertime, when the evening hours hum and buzz with particular intensity. Insects and butterflies fairly dominate the first act. (In his biography, *Prodigal Son*, Edward Villella complained that Balanchine barely had time to set his variation as Oberon, so preoccupied was he in working out the moves for the children.) One of the most moving moments in the ballet is when the baby insects, obeying the call of Mendelssohn, settle down for a night's sleep. They are followed by the butterflies, obedient to the silent call of Puck. Hark, he says, it is time to rest. At least the insect world is in harmony with nature. Nobody else is, of course, and that's the other theme of the first act of this two-act ballet, Balanchine's first original full-evening work.

Balanchine presents the cast of characters and their troubles in one breath. Within six minutes, a sorrowful Helena walks across the stage absent-mindedly plucking a leaf from Puck's invisible (to her) hand. Oberon and Titania fight over the changeling boy. Tipsy rustics galumph. Oberon and Titania have another fight. Then the scene switches from the forest to the court in Athens, where Theseus and Hippolyta hear the complaints of Hermia, Lysander, Helena, and Demetrius. Demetrius lunges toward Hermia. Rudely stamping his foot, he demands, Why can't I have her? Theseus dismisses them all with a disgusted wave of the hand. Now back to the forest, where Helena resumes her sad, dazed walk. The insects try to comfort her, but to no avail, and so lulled by Mendelssohn's lullaby they go to sleep.

Whereas Ashton's *The Dream* progresses logically, Balanchine's ballet begins as a jumble of events. But then, Shakespeare's play is about jumbles. Although the scenes are staged in sequence, they could be happening simultaneously, particularly the arguments between Oberon and Titania and the dance of the rustics. (Does Balanchine mean to equate the rustics' antics with the dispute between the king and queen of the fairies? Likely so, I think.) Balanchine also takes us backward and forward in time with cinematic speed. First, Helena is in the forest, next in Athens, next in the forest again.

In preparing a libretto for *The Dream*, Ashton wanted to stick to the main points of the story. Conciseness was usually Balanchine's approach as well, but in *Midsummer* he cast his net wider than Ashton does by including the characters of Theseus and Hippolyta (who has a long dance of her own in the first act). I think he decided to bring them into the proceedings to show that disorder ruled not only the enchanted forest but civil life as well. Theseus is the Duke of Athens; the four lovers appearing before him at his palace care not a whit for his authority.

Throughout the first act, the problems among the mortal lovers are comically conceived with well-timed gesture, all in pantomime. Demetrius is a lout, and Lysander stupid. The women, however, are portrayed with more sympathy. Helena's solo of lament is rather generic, but one truly feels for the abandoned Hermia during her long solo, when, lost in the forest, she twists and turns as if losing her mind.

The discord between Oberon and Titania is harder to read, having a quality not of the rustics' nonsense but of mindlessness. The key here is the fact that they repeat their claims for the little boy with exactly the same gestures and affect. The repetition makes their argument a ritual exercise, habitual, ingrained. This is the kind of couple whose natural mode is disharmony. Their reconciliation, after Titania emerges from her dream, is perfunctory; that is, they walk off the stage together. They do not dance a pas de deux, as they do in Ashton's version.

The great moment in *The Dream* is the duet between Oberon and Titania, the subtlest evocation of erotic love in all ballet literature. In *Midsummer* the two, as I have written, have no pas de deux. To music swelling with grandeur (the Overture to *Athalie*), music that could well serve as a grand pas de deux for Titania and Oberon, she dances instead with an unnamed cavalier. Her other duet is with Bottom. Ironically, this pas de deux between an adoring Titania and an uncomprehending donkey is set to the same music Ashton uses for his Titania/Oberon tryst. This impassioned music (the Nocturne from the incidental music to the play) is perfectly attuned to the sexual complexities that the two fairies ultimately resolve—his need to contain her independence and her need to resist. The Nocturne music also brings out the comic nature of the Titania/Bottom story: all that musical urgency bestowed upon an animal!

The story is simple: Titania loves Bottom and Bottom loves grass. Their impasse is encapsulated in the moment when Titania, in a swoon, bares her bosom to the animal while he responds by staring blankly at the audience. I, for one, associate that stare with the Jack Benny look, and that's because Balanchine loved Jack Benny. I know this because I remember an interview in which he responded to a question about his reputation by saying something like, "I'm overrated. Shakespeare is overrated. Mozart. Stravinsky. Even Jack Benny is overrated." In any case, Bottom's steadfast dumbness in the face of amorous longing always draws a laugh from the audience. Their duet is comedy at its sweetest.

Oberon's solo, danced to the scherzo, is the dance climax of Act I. With its speed and space-devouring thrust, it is a technical marvel and is consid-

New York City Ballet. Wendy Whelan as Titania and Kipling Houston as Bottom. *A Midsummer Night's Dream.* Choreography by George Balanchine © The George Balanchine Trust. Photo by © Costas.

ered one of the most challenging roles in the City Ballet repertory. Villella, for whom Oberon was created, summed up the technical paradox of the variation by writing that in preparation for the jumps, the *plié* had to be fully articulated, which means that you have to dance slower to dance faster.

The curious aspect about this first act is that, although the mortals make up, the hero and heroine go their separate ways. Thus no love pas de deux, thus no revelatory moment for the ballerina, the figure through whom Balanchine typically expresses his most profound feeling. But there is Act II to set things right.

Ashton could wrap up the story in one act and within the boundaries of

Mendelssohn's incidental music for Shakespeare's play. Balanchine needed a second act. Set at the court of Theseus in Athens, it is a wedding divertissement for the quartet of now-reconciled lovers, Theseus and Hippolyta, and a large ensemble. By choreographing a pure-dance final act Balanchine was following a time-honored convention from the nineteenth century. A second act also gave him the opportunity to use more and less familiar Mendelssohn, whom he much admired. By the time *Midsummer* is over, we have heard, in addition to the famous incidental music to the play,

New York City Ballet. Edward Villella as Oberon. *A Midsummer Night's Dream.* Choreography by George Balanchine © The George Balanchine Trust. Photo, Jerome Robbins Dance Division, The New York Public Library for the Performing Arts, Astor, Lenox and Tilden Foundations.

overtures to *Athalie, The Fair Melusine, The First Walpurgis Night,* and *Son and Stranger,* and the *Symphonia No. 9 for Strings.* But the main reason for Act II is to enable Balanchine to interpret the play in his own way.

For it is in the second act that we see the sublime pas de deux so markedly absent from the first. It is performed not by the fairy king and queen, as it would be in Shakespeare's play were it a ballet, but by an anonymous man and woman. In this duet the couple dance in slow whispers. He wafts her in low lifts forward and back. He slowly lifts her and places her down in quarter-turn rotations so that we can see her rest in always-changing perspectives, each of them utterly precious because of the deliberate softness with which the man carries her. He escorts her in a long diagonal of *bourrées,* her body quietly weaving left and right and so entwining us all in a spell. At the end, she falls backward into his arms, then way forward so that her chest almost touches the floor. From there he revolves her in a half-circle into the traditional swoon with which many romantic pas de deux conclude.

The partnering is tricky, but in this duet the mechanics are invisible. Act I is all push and pull, but here you don't know who is leading and who is following. When a hand is needed for support, it materializes out of thin air. It thus becomes a metaphor of trust and intimacy between two people. And compared to everything else that's come before, in Act II as well as Act I, it is so quiet and tender—so at home with itself. As one watches the duet, everything and everybody recedes into the distance. All that matters are these two dancers. Shakespeare said that the mortals are fools. Balanchine says that the whole lot of them are, except, of course, this one couple who dance the pas de deux. There is a streak of darkness in this comic ballet.

Obviously, it's crucial to Balanchine's game plan that the ballerina in the duet and Titania are not the same person, and in my experience they never have been. Once, though, at the end of a talk I had given on this ballet, the wife of the artistic director of the company I was visiting approached me with a twinkle in her eye. She told me that many years ago, when she was dancing with a troupe in Switzerland, Balanchine came for a few days to oversee the final rehearsals of the ballet. He was so taken with the dancer who performed Titania that he had her dance the pas de deux as well. He wanted to see her dance as much as possible in the short time he was there. Well, so much for my theory about the ballet's meaning. I guess the story shows that Balanchine was more interested in dancers than in ideas. Still, was it perverse of him to wreck the structure he had carefully built? Perhaps he was playing Puck.

It happens that Puck is the character who ends *Midsummer*. In *The Nutcracker* Balanchine chose to end the story in the Land of Sweets instead of returning to the reality of Marie's home. In *Midsummer*, though, he leaves the equivalent of the Land of Sweets to go back home to the forest. After the long divertissement—with its expansive (and sometimes dull) dancing and abundance of tutus—Mendelssohn's incidental music returns and so do the insects, who once again scurry about. Titania and Oberon join hands in a symbolic gesture of reconciliation, then parade off in opposite directions with their respective retinues. The lights grow darker, and Puck emerges from the shadows. The last we see of him, he's flying into a night sky sparkling with fireflies.

Jewels

1967

Before *Jewels* was a ballet, it was a marketing strategy. With unprecedented shrewdness from a company that supposedly disdained publicity, the City Ballet primed its audience for a hit: *Jewels* was to be ballet de luxe. The Fifth Avenue shop Van Cleef & Arpels was drawn into the act as Balanchine was photographed looking at a few of the store's magnificent, expensive necklaces and then explaining to the press that as a man of Georgian blood he had always admired jewelry. He also said that *Jewels* was not about jewels; it was about dancing. But those honest words somehow got lost in the buzz. How could they not, considering the dissemination of absolutely gorgeous formal portraits of Balanchine surrounded by the ballet's four ballerinas: Violette Verdy, Mimi Paul, Patricia McBride, and Suzanne Farrell. Looking a bit of the dandy, Balanchine wore a bemused expression conveying the idea that he possessed something more precious than emeralds, rubies, and diamonds. At his fingertips were four exquisite women, dressed in Karinska's exquisitely crafted headpieces and bejeweled bodices. Even today, these photographs are the epitome of glamour.

It was not the first time, in 1967, that the master of the domain would have been able to surround himself with such female allure. In the 1930s he had his "baby ballerinas." The 1950s had a surplus of distinct, glamorous personalities, beginning with Maria Tallchief. But as an encapsulation of the City Ballet's star power in the 1960s, those photographs are iconic.

As part of the publicity drive, *Jewels* was given first-ever hype, proclaimed as the first plotless full-length ballet. I can't imagine that this fact was a ticket-seller, but what do *I* know? Companies today still boast of it in their advertisements. Besides, it's not exactly true. The three ballets that make up *Jewels* do run for a full evening, but to my mind there is no idea uniting them beyond the jewels motif. Some writers feel that each section illustrates a national approach to classical dancing—French, American, and Russian. But these categories are too general to hold water. In *Jewels* Balanchine, as always, expressed the particularities of a score, in this ballet by Fauré, Stravinsky, and Tchaikovsky. In any case, nowadays each ballet is sometimes performed on its own, especially *Rubies*.

Nor was it the first time that Balanchine used the jewels idea. In the original version of *Symphony in C*—called *Le Palais de Crystal* at its premiere in 1947 for the Paris Opera Ballet—each of the four movements was costumed in the color of gems. (Unlike the Paris Opera ballet, *Jewels* has no sapphire section, although Kirstein wrote that Balanchine had pondered a blue ballet to Schoenberg.)

If *Jewels* was special, it was the choreography's intensely close response to the personalities of the women gazing out at us in the photographs. The pictures might have also included Edward Villella, so molded is *Rubies* to his personality. But he is understandably missing from the portrait gallery. His inclusion would have spoiled the unspoken assumption of the gathering: that, in Balanchine's dictum, "Ballet is woman."

Appreciation of just how perfectly Balanchine fit the dancing to the dancers developed in retrospect rather than during the first performances. I don't think it nostalgic to feel that *Jewels* was never the same after the original cast retired. The *Diamonds* section, to Tchaikovsky, has weathered time the best. Even though Farrell's sense of modest Imperial grandeur was unique, the ballet's genre and its strict classical language make it the most impersonal of the trio. *Rubies*, to Stravinsky, still has snap, but Villella's charm, McBride's vivacity, and both of their abilities to keep us in suspense about what would happen next in their duets have yet to be duplicated (in my experience, at least). *Emeralds*, to Fauré, is all but lost, despite Balanchine's refashioning of the Mimi Paul solo for dancers who had not her mysteriousness. The truth is that most everything I have to say about *Emeralds* is drawn from memory; it is not what one sees today. On the other hand, it remains the most fascinating and beautiful. And the de luxe aura in which the whole ballet bathes continues to be a box-office draw. At its premiere, in the spring of 1967, it was exactly the hit the company was hoping for—sold-out houses that satisfied everyone, including the scalpers.

Emeralds

Ironically, the extravaganza for which the audience was primed opens with a ballet that is inward. The critic Robert Garis said rightly that while *Rubies* and *Diamonds* lay out familiar territory, in *Emeralds* Balanchine invented a new world. As usual, one must look to the music as a source of his vision. *Emeralds* marked the first time Balanchine set a ballet to Fauré—selections from the suite *Pelleas and Melisande* and *Shylock*, rarely performed music composed for a play by Edmond de Haraucourt after Shakespeare. In describing *Emeralds*, Violette Verdy spoke of its "nostalgia" and feeling of "resignation." (And Verdy, unlike her successors in the role, made one understand the nobility of that feeling.) Even in the moments when the horns dominate, in the first ensemble dance, rather than hark to the future as horns are wont to do, they fall back on themselves and dissolve into resignation. The Fauré sound is autumnal, reminiscent of that of his contemporary, across the Channel, Elgar.

Drifting past us on air currents, rather than meter, *Emeralds* seems to happen partly out of view, as though a shifting cloud cover separates the dancers from the audience. The atmosphere is one of restraint. The two principal women hold their arabesques low, while the ensemble raises their legs not once. Lifts end in deep *pliés*, like sighs. The women swoon. They hold dialogues with themselves. All is quiet, sometimes hushed. Sometimes one dare not breathe, lest one violate the thick silence on stage. I am thinking especially of the most extraordinary part of *Emeralds*, the pas de deux for the Mimi Paul character and her cavalier, played in the first years by Francisco Moncion. All it is is a walk. The woman steps onto pointe slowly, reflectively, and self-absorbed. Although the couple walks arm in arm, she is unaware of him. We don't know what she is thinking, nor can we know. She moves in a cocoon. Several times the couple raises their arms and the woman her leg in upward notches, as though marking the passing of time or, perhaps, the inner, hidden pulse of Fauré's music. These relatively sharp moments interrupt the dream, but not for long. The couple resumes their

New York City Ballet. Conrad Ludlow and Violette Verdy. *Emeralds*. Choreography by George Balanchine © The George Balanchine Trust. Photo, Jerome Robbins Dance Division, The New York Public Library for the Performing Arts, Astor, Lenox and Tilden Foundations.

walk, and at the conclusion of the dance they walk off the stage as they came on, spellbound.

The solo for Paul, to the most familiar part of *Pelleas and Melisande*, contains a motif as insulated as her duet. She bows to one side, then the other, but to whom she is bowing remains unknown. If she is bowing to an audience, it is in her mind's eye. Does that make the real audience seated in the theater voyeurs? No, but it does make us privy to something private and out of our experience.

Balanchine rechoreographed the solo in the 1970s because, some dancers say, the conductor Robert Irving played the music too quickly for Balanchine's taste and wouldn't change the tempo. Thus, Balanchine

New York City Ballet. Mimi Paul and Francisco Moncion. *Emeralds.* Choreography by George Balanchine © The George Balanchine Trust. Photo, Jerome Robbins Dance Division, The New York Public Library for the Performing Arts, Astor, Lenox and Tilden Foundations.

changed the choreography to suit Irving's tempo. I don't buy the story completely. I think he changed it to better suit the dancers who replaced Paul after she had left the company. Only something of its elusiveness remains.

The solo for the Verdy character invites the audience into her world. (I call the Verdy and Paul parts characters because they indicate full and distinct lives as well as moods.) Thus it is different from the Paul solo, but its opening passage has all the mystery for which *Emeralds* is famous. The dance begins with a long passage of *ports de bras* as intricate and idiosyncratic as Balanchine ever did. Its secret is that the ballerina does not dance with her arms; she dances to them and they to her as in a conversation. The delicacy with which her arms fold out and in, curl upward, and brush across her forehead seem to delight her. The refinement of her arms, and the practiced way in which they move at times suggest a lady at her toilette. Again, the scene seems enclosed in the dancer's mind. Although the solo becomes less intense and less particular to Verdy's refinement in her upper body as it expands into swift, swirling movements, the opening motif is the controlling image.

Following the two solos comes a sprightly pas de trois including a standard male solo with beats and turns. This section might strike one as out of synch with the prevailing quietude. I think it is, but it shows to what extent Balanchine favored contrast over continuity of tone. However, the finale of *Emeralds* is downright dissonant. Because of the music, it cannot become one of Balanchine's proverbial applause machines, but its unison dancing and the cheerful effect of that device always seemed contrived, forcing a happy ending on a sad story. In 1976 he added a new elegiac ending, which leaves the men, now alone, kneeling and looking into the distance. He also composed a new pas de deux for the Verdy dancer and her partner, which is stately and grave. In adding these dances he gave *Emeralds* clearer definition, just as he would later do with the Stravinsky Festival's *Baiser de la Fée*.

Rubies

When posing for photos at weddings and other such events, we ladies know how to hold our legs so that they look their prettiest. You simply bend one leg and turn it in ever so slightly, thus creating a graceful curve and longer line in the thigh. Balanchine knew all about good legs. He once told a story about himself to show that he knew better than anyone else about legs. He and Richard Rodgers were auditioning a prospective chorus line for the musical *On Your Toes*. The ladies all wore high heels, which of course slims and elongates the legs. Rodgers thought the women were all gorgeous and was ready to hire them on the spot. Wait a minute, said

Balanchine, and ordered the women to stand in a line without their heels. Rodgers was flabbergasted at the difference. With merry eyes, Balanchine said, "You see, I know."

Balanchine also knew about the chorine's sweet/saucy attitude and the social dances of the time, because he had worked on Broadway musicals and Hollywood films. Between 1936 (*On Your Toes*) and 1944 he had contributed to thirteen musicals and a half-dozen films. Except for the *Slaughter on Tenth Avenue* ballet from *On Your Toes*, none of the choreography survives, but the spirit of the era inhabits such ballets as *Who Cares?* (1970), to Gershwin, and *Rubies*, to Stravinsky's 1928 *Capriccio for Piano and Orchestra*. In later times Bob Fosse would make the pelvic thrusts and turned-in legs and general jazzy look of the earlier era more stark, emphatic, and sour. Sometimes, in some performances, Fosse infiltrates the spirit of *Rubies*, but it's off the mark. With Stravinsky leading the way, *Rubies* is all high jinks and wit and playfulness. One thinks of the girls' scrunched up arms, like chicken wings; or the cakewalk strut of the ballerina and her cavalier, which they then reverse into a game of jump rope; and most of all the merry chase that the cavalier takes his four pals on. Of course they can't keep up with him—who could keep up with Villella—but that's the point.

Another aspect of the ballet's playfulness is Balanchine's adjustments of standard postures and steps in order to give them a jazzy, angular look in the mode of Stravinsky. The chorus girl's turned-in leg is the basic stance of the women in *Rubies*, but for the female soloist he exaggerates the line to almost outrageous proportion simply by jutting the bent leg out, as far away from the standing leg as possible. The gracious *balancé*, which opens *Diamonds*, becomes in *Rubies* a rocking motion with the pelvis leading. The *pas de bourrée* is a hootchy-kootch maneuver. The *emboîté* transforms into the cakewalk step. And those chicken-wing arms—how far from and how close they are to the swan's undulating arms. These little adjustments to the traditional vocabulary run rampant in *Rubies*, making the ballet a veritable textbook example of the device.

Balanchine often configures his leading dancers as "the one" versus "the two." In some works the soloist is a soubrette. Occasionally the lone figure is a man. In *Rubies* "the one" is a woman of formidable size, approaching the Amazonian prototype. (At least this is how Balanchine envisaged her,

New York City Ballet. Edward Villella. *Rubies*. Choreography by George Balanchine © The George Balanchine Trust. Photo, Jerome Robbins Dance Division, The New York Public Library for the Performing Arts, Astor, Lenox and Tilden Foundations.

although some companies don't have this physical type of dancer on their rosters.) Because she is a big girl, everything she does is hyperbolic. Her chorus-girl stance is in extremis. She doesn't walk; she strides. Her *pliés* in second position are so wide and deep they're a statement: here I am and you better believe it. There's so much of her, she needs four men to partner her. The soloist woman in the Choleric movement of *The Four Temperaments* is her antecedent, but the *Rubies* woman isn't angry; she's just big and strong.

What I find intriguing about the two and the one configuration is that it's a kind of world view. The couple and the soloist occupy inviolate spaces; in *Rubies* they don't dance together until the last minutes of the finale. A pas de trois would be a breach of their identities. So the couple (in Balanchine-land, always a man and woman) and the soloist are separate, but are they equal? I think not. Generally, in all of Balanchine's ballets there's an implicit hierarchy between the woman who does the pas de deux and the woman who doesn't. The coupled woman's persona tends to be enriched and expanded by dancing with a man. She is a sexual creature, while the solo figure is not. It's interesting to note that the Lilac Fairy in *The*

Sleeping Beauty has no partner; she's a major player but she's just a fairy. For her to dance a pas de deux would put her too close to Princess Aurora, who represents the complete person. In Balanchine's works the soloist always carries the ranking of bridesmaid. She may have some terrific dancing to do, but, sorry, no cigar.

If there was any single part of *Jewels* that turned it into a smash hit, it was the pas de deux in *Rubies*. You simply don't know what extraordinary thing is going to happen next in this encounter between the frolicsome lass and her virile partner. One second, she's plunging forward with all her weight, so that her face touches the floor. Next second, she's in a backbend. One second, she stands upright on pointe. The next, she's practically sitting on the floor, with one leg thrust in front of her, then the other. There are moments of respite from the precariousness, when the couple slinks forward and back (another variation on the leisurely *balancé* that opens *Diamonds*) or tries out a bit of social dancing. Then they're back at their cantilevered tricks again, defying the central axis on which mortals usually

New York City Ballet. Patricia McBride and Edward Villella. *Rubies.* Choreography by George Balanchine © The George Balanchine Trust. Photo, Jerome Robbins Dance Division, The New York Public Library for the Performing Arts, Astor, Lenox and Tilden Foundations.

move. Stravinsky's thumping piano adds exclamatory force, and sometimes a bit of lowdown and dirty humor, which Balanchine picks up in the passage where the man rocks his lady side to side, a little forward and back, while she's in a deep *plié* in second position, straddling his leg. It's one of the simpler moves in the duet, yet utterly arresting for its combination of sexiness and humor. That wide second position of hers makes you smile because there's something ungainly about it, but a good *Rubies* dancer carries it off with aplomb.

I remember well the first years of *Rubies*, when one watched the duet with bated breath and open mouth. It seemed the apotheosis of acrobatic bravura with a tinge of elegance coming from McBride's delicately held fingers and queenly trots around the stage, like a Lipizzaner. Villella's mix of virility and charm was his unique gift. But I think the duet's general loss of heat has to do with technique. McBride and Villella gave every movement and the split-second transitions between them complete articulation. They danced their hearts out. There was no holding back. McBride once said that she'd jump off a bridge for Balanchine. In *Rubies* she did, and bounced right back.

Diamonds

Balanchine didn't always choreograph a ballet in the sequence in which it is performed. Often he began with a pas de deux. In *Diamonds* he created the last, polonaise, movement first in order, he said, to know where he was going. He was going toward a show of force, a grand spectacle for sixteen couples plus the lead couple. This particular spectacle, however, does not have the ebullience, the heart-stopping splendor of other of his spectacles, such as *Vienna Waltzes* or *Symphony in C* or *Theme and Variations*, which like *Diamonds* is set to Tchaikovsky (his third symphony, minus the first movement). There's a certain gravitas pervading *Diamonds*, which finds its center in the *révérence* presented by the entire court. The ballet is more homage to than celebration of the Imperial age of Petipa, which Balanchine saw in its waning days. The fourth movement certainly ramps up the wattage of the preceding sections, but its politesse informs much of the rest of the ballet, especially the first and third parts. The second part, a long pas de deux of about ten minutes, is in a class by itself.

Maryinsky Ballet. *Diamonds*. Choreography by George Balanchine © The George Balanchine Trust. Photo by © Costas.

New York City Ballet. Suzanne Farrell and Jacques d'Amboise. *Diamonds*. Choreography by George Balanchine © The George Balanchine Trust. Photo by © Costas.

Politesse in the first movement, a slow waltz, translates as leisurely bordering on ponderous. Dressed in the full, drooping tutus reminiscent of those of the Imperial era, the ensemble of twelve women pose in the shape of a diamond, their *balancés* pressing into the first beat of the waltz rhythm rather than emphasizing the rebound in the second or third beats. The accent is down. That downward pressure is reflected in the women's pointe work as well. They don't spring lightly onto pointe in a *piqué* step, but rather roll up onto pointe in a *relevé*. Clearly, this first section is a prologue, but by Balanchine's standards an unusually slow-going one. It reminds me of Petipa's introductory ensemble dances for the peasants in *Swan Lake* or *Sleeping Beauty*. It is Balanchine working *in* the nineteenth century rather than off of it. The fact that the waltz is so deeply imbedded in nineteenth-century pace might explain why many people have said that you can't understand the waltz section until you've seen the corps of the Maryinsky Ballet dance it. (I haven't, alas.) From what I gather, the Russians settle into the downward drag of the waltz luxuriously, as though sinking into down pillows. They give it an amplitude, a bloom that Americans just can't muster.

The third, scherzo, movement is obviously lighter and quicker, yet Balanchine keeps the lid on. He doesn't duplicate the music's little flourishes in the woodwinds and strings with fleet, delicate footwork. He arches over the music, countering Tchaikovsky's scherzo with a measured, andante pace. Although the principals move with speed and fast turns, it's the ensemble passages that set the tone.

Suzanne Farrell wrote in her autobiography that when she first stepped onto the stage in the pas de deux, her guide was the "lonely" oboe that plays the adagio's major theme. Melancholy does indeed pervade the music, and so the dance. There's another kind of loneliness, too, which is odd considering the ardent attention paid to her by her partner. The ballerina in *Diamonds* moves in a kind of solitary splendor. She is not self-absorbed like the Paul character in *Emeralds*, but her movements, so grand and large, register like symbols of adagio dancing. This duet is a distillation of the pas de deux, and she is the messenger, the essence of the ballerina character. Her range is large—from the grand-scale *développés à la seconde*, the long supported promenades, and deep arabesques, to movements of great intimacy, as when she slowly walks on pointe with soft, yielding knees, giving her journey a slow-motion effect. (This pensive walking was a Farrell specialty.) Yet everything she does is measured, and so seems larger than it really is. One of my strongest images of the pas de deux is of the ballerina standing in a simple *passé* as she is promenaded in a circle by her partner. Yet she fills the space around her in this modest pose. It's all about the physical beauty of her line and her psychological composure.

Many people feel that the quintessential ballerina is the Swan Queen. There are indeed references to *Swan Lake* in this adagio, for much of it suggests flight and return and something in between, as when the ballerina runs away from the man while looking back at him, bidding him to follow her. The Swan Queen nestles in the swanness of her undulating arms, and the *Diamonds* ballerina's arms also move sensuously, as when her back hand delicately grazes the back of her head. (This particular placement of the arms is typically Eastern European, and it's a way of acknowledging the popular name of the third symphony, the Polish symphony.) *Diamonds*, however, tells no love story except perhaps of Balanchine's love for the character of the ballerina, who in 1967 was Suzanne Farrell. He didn't choreograph the duet first, but I think this is where he was going in *Diamonds*.

Valse Fantaisie

1967

A mere eight minutes long, *Valse Fantaisie* is a wisp of a ballet set to a composer who is rarely heard in today's concert halls. Yet Mikhail Glinka was a recurrent figure in Balanchine's career. More than his love for Tchaikovsky and Stravinsky, his love for Glinka identifies him specifically as Russian—not European or American—with loyalties to its monarchist heritage. Glinka was considered an emblem of Russian culture, like Pushkin, and his *A Life for the Tsar* is dubbed Russia's first national opera. Tchaikovsky and Stravinsky revered him, and Balanchine has said that he wrote "in true Imperial style."

As a student Balanchine danced in the opera *Ruslan and Ludmila* at the Maryinsky Theater. It was Glinka who lured Balanchine back to the stage as a dancer in 1950, when he choreographed for four couples the mazurka from *A Life for the Tsar*. I remember that he clicked his heels with great dash. His partner, however, Vida Brown, remembers being upset with him because he wouldn't stop snapping his fingers to mark the tempo.

It's the waltz, the *Valse Fantaisie*, that Balanchine couldn't let go of. He used it no fewer than four times, which is an all-time high for return visits to a particular score. The first *Valse* he created in 1931, in London, for Sir Oswald Stoll's variety show; a year later he put together a suite of Glinka pieces for the Ballet Russe de Monte Carlo. For his own New York City Ballet, in 1953, he set the *Valse* again for three ballerinas and a cavalier. This stayed in the repertory for almost a decade and was replaced with a second suite, *Glinkaiana*, in 1967. About a year later all but the *Valse Fantaisie* was dropped. And so this little gem of a waltz lives on.

It's precisely because it is short, small in scale—cast for a lead couple and four women—and simple in construction that it reveals so clearly Balanchine's craft. The effect he sought was delicacy, lightness, a feeling of being wind swept. He homed in on an extremely limited range of steps— fast waltz steps, skimming jumps that cover a lot of space, and for contrast little prances and runs. For even more contrast, he established as a motif a larger movement with more give—a soft lunge that for a second brings the dancers into contact with the floor. That lunge is the first thing the dancers

New York City Ballet. John Clifford and Mimi Paul. *Valse Fantaisie.* Choreography by George Balanchine © The George Balanchine Trust. Photo, Jerome Robbins Dance Division, The New York Public Library for the Performing Arts, Astor, Lenox and Tilden Foundations.

do, and as the contrasting element is supposed to do, it underscores the skimming delicacy of everything else.

Considering the small range of steps, the amount of variety Balanchine squeezed out of them is amazing. Notice all the different ways he deploys six people—solos, duets, four ladies and the gent, just the ensemble. There's one moment where each woman runs on by herself, a mini-solo. Sometimes the four women dance in unison, but often they're split into twos. The placement of the dancers is mostly horizontal, but once when the women line up vertically, with the ballerina in front, the effect is much larger than its substance; it's as if you'd never seen a vertical line before. The same kind of illusion with circles happens once as well. Most of the time the dancers move in big arcs, with plenty of breathing room between them. At one point, however, the four women make a small circle while the two principals dance in big circles around them. It's as if you'd never seen small before. The effect is of a bouquet of flowers, whose center is a nosegay of buds. The end result of this play with small differences is a ballet that instead of being repetitious is refreshing to the eye and spirit.

I have a memory of *Valse Fantaisie* that moves from craft to magic, for it eludes analysis. It is of Mimi Paul's dancing in the lead role when the ballet was first performed, in 1967—the moment when she circled the stage in quick *grands jetés*. She brought to these jumps an intensity, almost a fierceness that left one gasping and slightly stunned, because the feeling of the movement went way beyond the emotional parameters of the ballet. Everyone has precious memories of past performances, and they are all subjective. But the Mimi Paul moment is shared by many. One former dancer thinks that her intensity came from her struggle to jump; jumping was her one technical weakness. Another former dancer recounts a story about Paul and *Valse Fantaisie*. One day Balanchine asked Paul why she didn't take company class more often. She told him that he didn't give enough jumps in class, so she went elsewhere. Balanchine then said something like, "Oh, so you want jumps. Well dear, I'll make for you a little ballet with jumps." And so he did.

The Stravinsky Festival

1972

Between June 18 and 25, 1972, the New York City Ballet presented thirty-one ballets to Stravinsky's music. Twenty-two of them were premieres, nine of them by Balanchine. The statistics themselves attest to the daring of the Stravinsky Festival, but they cannot really describe the experience of attending it. As one watched the performances night after night, a heady momentum began to take hold. To some extent, what one actually saw on stage mattered less than that it was happening in the first place. The fact that the whole shebang was squeezed into a week gave the festival an accumulating intensity that, for the moment at least, took precedence over the merits and demerits of this and that premiere.

Clinkers there were plenty of, but a bit of strategic planning by Balanchine, who organized each night's repertory, ensured that each of the seven programs would have some measure of artistic substance—which is to say, six of the programs contained at least one new work by him, and all included Stravinsky ballets he had done before. His shrewdest move was to unveil the *Stravinsky Violin Concerto* and *Symphony in Three Movements* back to back on the first program. These were big ballets and although very different—the concerto tidy and the symphony sprawling—both were clearly major in intent and major in delivery. Some compared the feel of the festival to being on an ocean voyage with some twenty-five-hundred passengers seated in the New York State Theater. Opening night, however, was more like a blastoff. It was also a clarion call to those who had begun to wonder whether the master had lost his touch. Some critics used words like "phoenix" and "resurrection" to describe Balanchine's achievement in that opening program.

These words were an overstatement, although like all exaggerations they had a foundation in reality. A year before the festival, Balanchine had created *PAMTGG*, an acronym for "Pan Am Makes the Going Great," an advertising jingle. Now Balanchine had made so-so ballets before, but this one was a bona fide dud. (The title alone was enough to set off warning signals.) He knew it was no good, but even before the curtain went up it was already a thing of the past. According to his assistant, Barbara Horgan, he was already dreaming up a tribute to his friend and muse, Stravinsky, who had just died, and on the night of the *PAMTGG* fiasco was outlining to Horgan a plan to present a week of nothing but Stravinsky the following June.

The Pan Am ballet aside, the years preceding the festival had been relatively fallow. Some thought that Balanchine was suffering over the departure of his adored Suzanne Farrell, who was more or less forced to decamp in 1969. Symptoms of his lovesickness could be seen in the morose atmosphere of his *Tschaikovsky Suite No. 3* and, some thought, in his perverse decision to stage *Les Sylphides* (renamed to its original title of *Chopiniana*) without the ballet's famous tulle skirts and with some dubious casting. On the other hand, there was *Who Cares?*, a blithe tribute to George Gershwin, and a delightful but modest *La Source* to Delibes. Still, they were not the best of years, and it's also true that those years were dominated by Jerome Robbins, who created *Dances at a Gathering* and *The Goldberg Variations*. Nevertheless, the spectacular success of the Balanchine wing of the Stravinsky Festival was no surprise. Since 1928 Stravinsky had been firing Balanchine's imagination; between *Apollo* and the festival Balanchine had set ballets to eighteen of his scores. There was little chance that Stravinsky would let him down in 1972.

Given the brouhaha of the festival in general and Balanchine's contribution to it in particular, it is natural to ponder how his major works of 1972 have fared over time, under normal circumstances. Which of those ballets—*Stravinsky Violin Concerto*, *Symphony in Three Movements*, *Duo Concertant*, and *Divertimento from Baiser de la Fée*—best bear the test of repeated viewings? I would venture to say *Baiser*, although it is the most flawed of the group—that is, until Balanchine modified it in 1974. As I wrote in the essay on *Agon*, Balanchine tended to move away from the traditional classical vocabulary in his later responses to Stravinsky. He seemed to care less about the inherent viability and beauty of traditional *pas* in favor of finding kinetic moves matching the musical pulse of *Duo Concertant* and *Violin Concerto* and the sheer scale of the symphony.

I think it all boils down to this: I'd rather see steps than moves, an *emboîté* instead of a prance, an arabesque instead of a leg kick. That's why I like ballet in the first place—to see all those codified pas; and why I love Balanchine best of all—because he recombines them and presents them in different contexts with unsurpassed nuance. Stravinsky composed *Baiser de la Fée* in homage to Tchaikovsky, and in its lyricism and beguiling mysteriousness the music is indeed Tchaikovskian. Thus, Balanchine's *Baiser* is inevitably the most classically minded. There is more to see.

Symphony in Three Movements

Symphony in Three Movements is one of Balanchine's trademark black-and-white ballets—practice costumes, contemporary music, angular movement—except that this one is black, white, and pink (to be precise, three shades of pink). The pink leotards, worn by the three female principals, were added some time after the premiere and after several experiments with color for the other women in the ballet as well. The pink was a kind of color-coding to set off the leading ladies from the ensemble. Normally, Balanchine doesn't need color to distinguish the soloists from the crowd. He sets up his hierarchies of dancers—principals, soloists, demi-soloists, and ensemble—through use of space. *Symphony in Three Movements*, however, is a sprawling and, so it seemed at the premiere, rather messy avalanche of movement. Propelled by restless entrances and exits of dancers who spring all over the stage, their spatial relationships always in flux, the ballet is anarchic. Sometimes you get the feeling that some of the dancing is pushing beyond the stage into a place the audience can't see. And at one point during the last movement, the feeling becomes reality: the ensemble is indeed only half visible as they step in and out of the wings.

The curtain opens on a misleading note. A long diagonal of women poses with lovely arched backs and open arms, stunning in their symmetry. Ah, a *ballet blanc* to Stravinsky, just what he had wanted for his *Apollo*. Then the composer's first chords blare out, and the *ballet blanc* association turns *noir*. The women swing their arms violently in big circles, fling them upward and plunge forward, their heads lowered and arms thrown in front

New York City Ballet. *Symphony in Three Movements*. Heather Watts, Bart Cook, Maria Calegari, Joseph Duell. Choreography by George Balanchine © The George Balanchine Trust. Photo by © Costas.

of them. As if in response to this demonic invocation, the first of the male principals leaps from the wings, making big but disconnected thrusts and jumps. Soon he is joined by a woman, and no sooner has she entered than they're both off, setting the stage for the entry of another woman. She dances in the middle of a small ensemble—a moment of respite—then starts turning furiously fast through two lines of women who are charging at her. Off she spins . . . into outer space? No time to ponder that, because the next man and entourage bound on, soon followed by a third couple.

The movements of the principals and demi-soloists (at least, I think that's what they are) are choppy and for the men in particular unnatural, because they drive themselves down to the ground from a jump before they have completed the jump's natural upward course. Perhaps Balanchine meant to block the music's propulsion with choreography that proceeds in fits and starts. Simultaneously, though, the music's drive is expressed by the ensemble, who strut and step with their backs in a crouch, arms flailing, and ponytails swinging. Their insistent stepping makes a background hum, slightly menacing because it is background noise. And the fact that they step bent-legged on pointe makes them *very* scary, because there is nothing as piercing as a pointe shoe hitting the floor on a bent knee.

Like everyone else, the ensemble has been on and off stage throughout the first movement. At the end they regroup into their original diagonal, and the man who first jumped onto the stage returns again, jumping. Is Balanchine about to bring the chaos to resolution? Looks like it, except for one small matter. The diagonal of ladies splits into two by a pace, so that you're not sure if the line is jagged by mistake or intent. It is unsettling, and so is the ensuing metamorphosis of the women's bodies. One by one, they suck in their outflung arms and legs and unfurl themselves into an open position, their faces uplifted toward the audience. We're back to *ballet blanc* beauty, except that there is something eerie about their transformation. It's like watching flowers bloom in reverse. I think this is the most stunning and disturbing image of the ballet.

The second movement, a pas de deux, is marked andante, but because it follows the sound and fury of the first part, its tempo seems almost as if at a standstill. Perhaps this effect is also due to the trancelike attitude of the two dancers. Their bodies are intimate with each other, yet they hardly seem aware of each other. They cut exotic poses, but to what ends? Are they Indian dancers, figures on a totem pole? Sometimes their duet is suffused with Far Eastern coloration, perhaps because their legs are often bent. Underneath their trancelike state is a hint of the barbaric, but accounting for this would touch on a great mystery of Balanchine's art. Does the choreography feel the way it does because of the music, or does the music sound the way it does because of the choreography? I hear something fierce and primitive going on. Stravinsky wrote that although this music, written between 1942 and 1945, is not programmatic, it was influenced by newsreels he saw of the war and more generally by the brutality of the times. In this second section perhaps we hear and see violence subterranean.

The last movement returns to high gear. There is a moment of relative quiet when the six soloists "speak" to each other in quick canonic interplay off to the side of the stage. (In this ballet, it's when dancing takes place stage center that you are surprised.) But this settling down serves only as a revving up for the most bizarre passage of the ballet. The ensemble retreats to the edges of the wings, so that their bodies are half visible. As the music presses on with great urgency, like huge machines rolling inexorably forward, the women repeatedly take big steps into full view and then stride back behind the wings. Their legs are bent on pointe, and their arms sweep back and forth across their faces like windshield wipers. Maybe they're robots; maybe latter-day Wilis. Then the idea is dropped abruptly as the stage fills with the entire cast of thirty-two. Everyone dances in unison—always reassuring and exhilarating—and then comes another sign of danger. The men rush forward and fall to the floor, poised to invade the audience. The women space themselves across the stage; a few raise their arms upward, a few others to the side. Having now created what looks to me like a Klee canvas, the dancers freeze while Stravinsky drives on. The music has the last word.

People who saw *Agon* in its earliest performances remember that the dancers' insecurity with the difficult score and choreography gave an added edge to the already edgy ballet. In later years they missed that extra tension

New York City Ballet. *Symphony in Three Movements*. Choreography by George Balanchine © The George Balanchine Trust. Photo by © Costas.

as the dancers became more comfortable with their parts. The early performances of *Symphony in Three Movements* also benefited from the dancers' unease with the ballet's wildness, disorder.

Today, it still spews energy at the audience, and the opening tableau never fails to elicit a gasp. There was one night, however, when the power of that tableau joined with a specific occasion to produce a theatrical event of its own. It was in 1977, the City Ballet's first performance after a long orchestra strike. The audience booed the musicians as they took their seats in the pit, but as soon as the curtain went up the booing turned to applause. "We're back," the line of women seemed to declare in capital letters. As if taking its cue from the boldness of the tableau, the audience clapped louder. The conductor could not give the downbeat because the dancers would not have been able to hear the music. The clapping grew more intense. The audience seemed to want to say something, to leave a mark, to stage a demonstration: to shut down the orchestra as it had shut down the dancers? Meanwhile, the dancers were frozen in place. A few began to look into the wings, seeking guidance. The strong stance of the dancers began to falter, but still the audience would not quiet down. There was a stand-off. Then finally, finally, finally, the curtain came down. The demonstration stopped. The curtain went up again, and the ballet began. The episode was exhilarating, troubling, slightly dangerous. Just like *Symphony in Three Movements*.

Stravinsky Violin Concerto

Balanchine was reluctant to appraise his ballets publicly, but the *Stravinsky Violin Concerto* (*Concerto in D Major for Violin and Orchestra*) was an exception. He said that he was satisfied with it, that it was well made. During the preparations for the festival it received more rehearsals than any other ballet. The female leads, Kay Mazzo and Karin von Aroldingen, recalled that he lavished unusual care on the choreography, revising passages more than was his wont. However, Balanchine's rehearsal pianist, Gordon Boelzner, believed that all those rehearsals were not necessarily devoted to perfecting the work, but to give Balanchine more opportunities to hear the music, so much did he love it. (Indeed, this was his second go at the score; the first, called *Balustrade*, was made in 1941 for the Original Ballets Russes.) Yes, the score is marvelous, especially, to my ears, the second aria with its plaintive song of the violin.

The ballet shows great deliberation. You feel that every move is there for a purpose. It's spanking clean. Sometimes, though, Balanchine wants to move beyond elegance of construction into the realm of human relationships, which are less clean. This realm is typically channeled through pas de deux. The *Violin Concerto* has two of them, set to the two arias of the score. The first tells its tale with unusual explicitness; just about every move and configuration of the couple spells struggle. Here are a man and woman who spend a tremendous amount of energy thwarting each other by means of thwarting the natural laws of partnering. As their limbs interlock, they face away from each other, thus making what could be a simple, natural maneuver impossible. They struggle to unlock at the very moments when they are going through contortions to embrace. You could call the duet a comedy about crossed signals, except that the determination with which they pull and twist is almost painful to witness. At the end he promenades

New York City Ballet. Bart Cook and Karin von Aroldingen. *Stravinsky Violin Concerto*. Choreography by George Balanchine © The George Balanchine Trust. Photo by © Costas.

her (one instance where their hands actually touch) and then sinks to the ground onto his back while she towers above him. It's a no-win ending. One imagines the Siren and Prodigal Son years later when they are no longer seductress and fascinated novice, but two people plain worn out.

According to Louise Dushkin, the wife of Samuel Dushkin, for whom the violin concerto was written, she once saw Stravinsky weep as her husband played the music during a performance. Asked why the tears, the composer replied that the second aria was written as an apology to his wife for having a longtime love affair with another woman. To this sometimes tender, sometimes passionate music Balanchine created a dialogue that captures the vicissitudes, the emotional volatility of an intimate sexual relationship. She turns away; he comes to her side. Their arms join and slip apart in quiet unrest, then in harmony. Her sudden collapses are resolved, with her partner's care. In one of the duet's loveliest moments, they mark the pulse of the music with soft *balancés* as their intertwined arms trace thoughts in the air. It seems like a new chapter in their life together. But in a blink, the mood changes. So it goes between lovers.

As an essay on the variations in climate between intimates, this duet stands alongside the pas de deux in *Agon*. It is also, I think, a metaphor for the relationship between a ballerina and the choreographer, whose role is taken by the man. He's the one who activates her; he walks her, rotates her, steadies her, and presents her to the audience in interesting ways. She responds under his gentle authority. The partnership is fruitful because he manipulates her intelligently while she abandons herself to his expertise. She leans back against him and places one foot in front of the other with exquisite delicacy, while he turns her body so that she is approaching the audience at striking angles. He pivots her this way and that, showing us the multifaceted aspect of her line (much like Terpsichore presents herself to Apollo). When he is not by her, she is still; at one point she sits on the floor, her fingers touching her cheek. She waits, reflective and unworried.

The beauty of their dancing is that, although they move with total intimacy, the figures they cut are separate, sometimes in counterpoint. In the final passage, though, they fuse. He cradles her with one arm and slowly rocks her from side to side. His other arm reaches outward and draws in and is positioned so that it's hard to tell whose arm is moving, his or hers. (I was amused to learn that Peter Martins, who created the role, said that Balanchine described this tender gesture as "begging for money.") As al-

New York City Ballet.
Kay Mazzo and Peter
Martins. *Stravinsky Violin
Concerto*. Choreography
by George Balanchine ©
The George Balanchine
Trust. Photo by © Costas.

ways, the woman follows the man's lead willingly, one might say passively. The idea is clinched when, in the last moment, he stands behind her, tilts her head backward, and covers her eyes. She is sightless but not mindless, because she accedes to his manipulations with her own quiet will. She seems to be saying, "I will do this, and I will look beautiful." She does.

In these duets the vocabulary Balanchine uses is shaped by the stories he wants to tell. One watches the dancers for what they have to say as much as for what they do. The first and fourth movements are driven by that incessant musical pulse of Stravinsky's. The literalness with which Balanchine translates the music's beat into visual beats is unprecedented. Perhaps to give absolute immediacy to the connection between what one hears and sees, he moves away from codified *pas*; the dancers simply move with balletic elegance and clarity.

The structure of the first movement, the Toccata, is so clean and elegant that it supersedes what the dancers actually do. It is divided into eight parts. In the first two, each of the two female principals dances with four men (eight men in total). Then come the two male principals, each backed up by an ensemble of four women. Then the format repeats, except that each quintet is of the same gender. What keeps the whole thing buoyant is the whirlwind of entrances and exits, the surprising overlaps between arrivals and departures, and the slight differences between opposite-sex and same-sex groupings. There's also a tiny witticism that stamps the entire section with good humor. The whole ballet—and certainly the first and last parts—is about the gotta-dance energy of the music. So how does it begin? The curtain rises to reveal the first of the quintets, the music begins, and nobody moves. The music continues, and still nobody moves. And still and still . . . until *finally* the lead woman kicks her leg in a quasi-attitude. This is one way to bring the audience to the edge of their seats.

Even after many viewings, that delayed beginning still works its magic. So, too, does the contrasting calm of the final pose—a spacious, pretty formation of five men. It's a moment's respite from the preceding smallness and tick-tick-tick momentum, and it is very, very welcome.

The fabric of the last section is even smaller and tighter than the first. The idea, I think, is to create the illusion of movement via the dancers' syncopation with the music and counterpoint with each other. While the soloists are prancing and two-stepping up front, the ensemble is moving like a mass of body parts—shifting weight from one leg to the other, turning one knee inward and outward, rotating wrists palm outward, palm inward. *Symphony in C*, to Bizet, creates the same choral-versus-soloist tension when the ensemble does *tendus*, *battements*, and *ports de bras* at the stage's perimeters, while the soloists do pirouettes stage center. In the *Violin Concerto* we're down to rotating wrists in the back and quick walks up front.

Balanchine emphasizes in this last movement the Russianness of the music. With their arms folded over their chests as they make their very tiny steps, the principals sometimes look like Russian dolls on parade. One can imagine the ladies wearing the traditional Russian headdresses, as they do indeed in a miniature sequel to this last movement, the *Scherzo à la Russe*, another premiere during the Stravinsky Festival. This folk-Russian flavor is sometimes charming, sometimes overdone. A more delicious moment, to my mind, comes earlier on, when one of the male principals makes a tardy entrance, and everyone waves in greeting. This entrance, coming out of no-where in a ballet that above all prizes exactitude, makes one wonder if the "mistake" was inspired by a real mistake during rehearsal. One thinks of the chance events in rehearsals for *Serenade* that ended up in the choreography. I like to think it was, because it would indicate the high spirits Balanchine enjoyed while making the ballet.

Obviously, Stravinsky was not around to enjoy the craftsmanship of the ballet, but he did attend many rehearsals of the first ballet Balanchine made to the score, *Balustrade*. Stravinsky is on record for praising the work, although it received mixed reviews and was performed only three times.

One would assume that there are always similarities between ballets set to the same score, but in this case it's hard to imagine what they might be. The 1972 version has no décor or costumes. Pavel Tchelitchev, a fanciful artist with a bent toward the arcane, was in charge of *Balustrade*'s produc-tion, which means that décor and costumes were paramount, if not dis-tracting. We know that one section was an erotic, surreal trio for a woman (Balanchine's once-beloved Tamara Toumanova) and two men; and that the second aria was a solo for Toumanova. There was a hint of jazz in some of the movements. It was a ballet of many moods, changing unpredict-ably, perhaps fantastically. My hunch is that Balanchine was very much under the influence of Tchelitchev's love of the bizarre. The *Stravinsky Violin Concerto*, in contrast, is a direct communion between composer and choreographer.

Divertimento from Le Baiser de la Fée

Scores with a built-in libretto tended to hamper Balanchine's imagination. He preferred to invent stories—I use the word loosely—where none had been intended by the composer, such as in the two duets for *Stravinsky Violin Concerto*. *Le Baiser de la Fée* has a story imbedded in its notes, but Balanchine was drawn to it anyway. The story's theme, about the artist and his muse, was especially resonant. And the music itself—Stravinsky's Tchaikovskiana, Balanchine called it—was obviously dear to his heart. For the festival, Balanchine abandoned the complete score, about forty-five minutes long, for the *Divertimento*, or suite, which is about half as long as the full score.

With the *Divertimento from Le Baiser de la Fée* Balanchine got to have his cake and eat it too; that is, he was able to suggest a story without having to go into the details. It took him many productions and many years to achieve his preferred form, and even with the 1972 *Divertimento* version the work was not yet done. In 1974 he added an epilogue, and only then could one say that *Baiser* was a plotless narrative.

Stravinsky was commissioned to write *Le Baiser de la Fée* for Ida Rubinstein, whose company premiered it in 1928, in Paris, with choreography by the distinguished Bronislava Nijinska. Balanchine's first go at the score, in 1937, was for a program of three Stravinsky ballets he created at the Metropolitan Opera, where his American Ballet was in residence. In 1940 *Baiser* was danced by the Ballet Russe de Monte Carlo and revived six years later when Balanchine was the company's resident choreographer. In 1947 he set it for the Paris Opera Ballet, and in 1950 it entered his own New York City Ballet. Balanchine dropped it from the repertory two or three years later, then brought it back to life again for the 1972 Stravinsky Festival.

All five productions prior to 1972 were genuine story ballets based on Stravinsky's libretto, itself inspired by Andersen's *The Ice Maiden*. A child is abandoned by his mother in a snowstorm. A fairy implants a kiss on his cheek. Years later the baby, now a grown man, is engaged, and during the wedding festivities the fairy returns as a bride in a black dress and claims the man. In the final scene, she leads him into eternity. Stravinsky called his score an homage to Tchaikovsky, and incorporated much of his piano music and songs into the music. Stravinsky saw his libretto as an allegory of Tchaikovsky's life "by relating," he wrote, "the Fairy to his Muse . . . the Muse having similarly branded Tchaikovsky with her fatal kiss, whose mysterious imprint made itself felt in all this great artist's work."

The theme was a natural for Balanchine, but the production elements required by the libretto were a source of endless trouble. The main problem was how to stage the final scene, where the fairy leads the man to his death, or eternal bliss, depending on one's own viewpoint. In some productions, the man climbed through netting to reach the fairy. In one version, the epilogue took place behind a scrim bathed in eerie light. Another problem was how to effect complicated scene changes gracefully, for the ballet's format was not the traditional two- or three-acter, where one could bring the curtain down. Kirstein saw a basic clash between the Tchaikovskian music and the alpine setting upon which Stravinsky insisted. And so the whole project was finally scrapped, leaving the public with memories of superb dramatic moments and superb dancing, especially by Maria Tallchief as the Fairy.

For the 1972 divertimento version, Balanchine used no décor but did dress the women in tutus borrowed from a long-forgotten ballet called *Roma* (1955). The one man in the ballet wore a blue tunic with flowing sleeves, echoing the Poet's sleeves in *Les Sylphides*. Compared to the majority of Balanchine's other Stravinsky works, *Baiser* looked positively traditional and rather pretty. The dancing, too, especially the opening movement for the ensemble, is straight Balanchine classicism, marked here by delicate footwork and sprightly *pas de chat*. The pas de deux, which often becomes a ballet's center, is elusive, however. It's hard to find its tonal core, although it does have marvelous moments—the ballerina's dramatic plunge into a deep arabesque, her entwining embrace of the man with her

New York City Ballet. Megan Fairchild and Joaquin De Luz. *Divertimento from Le Baiser de la Feé.* Choreography by George Balanchine © The George Balanchine Trust. Photo by © Costas.

leg in attitude. If one feels a tension in their dancing, it's because of the music, I think, rather than the dancing. If one feels a similar tension in the ballerina's solo, it's because her timing is a hairsbreadth ahead of the music, not because her steps express a state of mind.

It's the man's solo that steers this cheerful little ballet way beyond the boundaries Balanchine has initially set. It begins with simple *tendus battements* and *ports de bras* reminiscent of the opening of the Tchaikovsky *Theme and Variations*, except that the man's body is at a slant, off kilter. Throughout the solo, normal movements are darkened by being off-center or done in convoluted sequences. When he turns in attitude his body leans away from his central axis and his eyes focus on his uplifted arm rather than straight ahead. He pirouettes to the ground, then turns in the opposite direction to his full height. It's all inside out and woozy-making. The music presses on, and the choreography becomes more febrile and unpredictable. One moment the man leaps in the air, the next he's leaning over, his arms lapping the floor. Suddenly there is a break in the music's drive, and the man sinks to the floor. Then he rises, reaches high into the air as though he is looking for something or thought something. He runs, jumps, sinks to the floor. He does it again, and again. Then he runs off the stage, leaving the audience feeling that it has seen the inside of a man's dream—a dream of quest, a foreboding of events?

In the finale the man's brief solo has all the strange inside-out qualities of the earlier solo, but this one is raised to virtuoso level. He does a series of low *grands jetés* around the stage, but instead of leaning forward into the line of direction, he throws his weight backward, seeming to push off his back leg. His momentum comes not from a natural forward drive but, it seems, from an unseen propeller pushing him from behind. Instead of facing the circular line of direction, his body is at an oblique angle to it. His weight pulls away from the center of the circle in which he travels, yet he maintains his flight route. The passage challenges one's own sense of equilibrium, and it's not easy for the dancer either. I remember Helgi Tomasson practicing this *manège* over and over after class during preparations for the Stravinsky Festival. I remember, too, a slight smile on his face, as though marveling at the perversity of the passage as well as its inventiveness.

The finale concludes with standard Balanchinian methodology. The ensemble moves with clear, strong legs and, divided into two groups, in emphatic and exciting canonic dialogue. The principals leap on, and everyone dances in unison, ending with a big pose for the principals. It could be the finish of any number of upbeat ballets, except that the man's role has cast a shadow that the sunny finale cannot dispel.

Baiser isn't the only time that Balanchine dropped a troubling atmosphere into a ballet and walked away from it. Two years after the premiere, however, he decided to make good on the Tomasson solo. (I call it by the dancer's name because it is his forever, so thoroughly did Balanchine draw upon Tomasson's musicality, subtlety of expression, and technical gifts.) The added epilogue begins with the ensemble separating the man from the woman. The separation is one of those iconographic moments signaling that something is up. In a brief pas de deux, the woman, supported by her partner, walks backward on pointe; she leans so far back that she cannot see where she is going. These "blind" walks are another of Balanchine's indications that the hand of fate hangs in the air. The couple embraces and separates. The ensemble now files on in slow *bourrées* and glides between

New York City Ballet. Helgi Tomasson. *Divertimento from Le Baiser de la Feé.* Choreography by George Balanchine © The George Balanchine Trust. Photo by © Costas.

the couple, separating them again and again. The ensemble then forms a diagonal line, and as its dancers slowly bend side to side, like willow trees in the breeze, the man and woman look for each other through the line. The women file off, leaving the couple alone. The two walk slowly toward opposite wings, their torsos arched backward so that they cannot see where they are going. The curtain falls.

Truth is, in the first two years of *Baiser*'s life I don't remember being unsatisfied with the zippy ending. You wondered about all the troubled undercurrents in the man's solos and the fact that they were so different from the rest of the ballet, but so be it. The new ending, however, made *Baiser* a coherent experience. And it seemed the perfect solution to all the dissatisfactions that Balanchine felt about the ending of his earlier productions. You don't need nets and scrims and what have you to express fate and loss and the open-endedness of eternity. A line of women gliding between a couple tells it all.

Duo Concertant

As the curtain goes up on *Duo Concertant* the gaze of the two dancers occasionally shifts from violinist to pianist and back again as they stand behind the piano at the side of the stage. That's all the dancers do—listen to the music. If there were any single personification of the Stravinsky Festival's intent, it was *Duo Concertant*. Without the distraction of choreography, the audience naturally listens to the music with unusual concentration. But there is a kind of choreography going on in the dancers' faces, and it draws one farther into the music. Their demeanor, pleasantly attentive but basically neutral in expression, arouses one's curiosity. They're very alert, but do they have thoughts? In wondering if and what thoughts are passing through their minds, one listens to the music even harder in order to discover one's own responses.

Perhaps they have been thinking that they'd like to dance, because that is what they do in the following four movements. You can see the dance take shape literally, layer by layer. First they move their arms up and down and from side to side, as if conducting. Then their legs move, then their torsos, then the woman rises on pointe and the man moves in to partner her. And we're off to the dance.

New York City Ballet. Yvonne Borree and Peter Boal. *Duo Concertant*. Choreography by George Balanchine © Kay Mazzo. Photo by © Costas.

In the ensuing pas de deux and two solos, the intimate relationship between the dancers and musicians is always maintained. For one thing, from time to time the dancers return to the piano or stop in mid-step to listen to the music. Once they hold hands as they listen; once the man slips his arm around his partner's waist. Sweet moments these are. The choreography, too, binds dancers and musicians, dance and music. Its repetitiveness creates a primal connection, an illusion of the music coursing through the dancers' blood and into their muscles, inspiring them to move.

The man's solo is more introspective than the woman's. At times he seems to be experimenting, trying on little jumps and *ports de bras* for size and recording how it all feels. Gradually his dancing grows more expansive: he does more and thinks less. The woman's solo, in contrast, is oriented toward the audience and makes the man's solo seem an etude. But in its repetition of simple phrases, it too cleaves to the music's pulse. And the fact that the pianist and violinist are right up there with the dancers makes the connection between music and dance even more palpable.

In the fifth and final section, everything changes. The dancers move far from the musicians to the other side of the stage. The lights darken. A spotlight falls on the musicians, and another one lights a small area in which the dancers will play out a drama of their own. The woman places her arm in the light, and the man hastens to it and links his arm with hers. He embraces her, sinks to his knees, and feels her face with his hands. She steps out of the light, then he does. She returns and again places her arm in the light. He comes back, kisses the back of her hand with hushed passion, then sinks to the floor like a supplicant before his ideal, here imagined as a beautiful arm in a beam of light.

The switch from youthful hand-holding to passionate caressing and from playfulness to intense questing is bold, if not brazen, and it is breath-taking. There is no preparation for this play within a play, no cue that Balanchine will break free of the music he has followed so closely and enter his own private fantasy. Yet because there are so many instances in which Balanchine shows us man and woman as servant and muse, this drama on the high seas rings true.

I had always wondered how Balanchine heard in this music such a romantic scenario. One day I came upon an old recording of Stravinsky and Samuel Dushkin playing the score. (Stravinsky composed the music, in 1932, with Dushkin in mind so that the two could take it on tour as part of a program of chamber-sized music. The tours were one of Stravinsky's money-making schemes.) Dushkin's violin playing was extremely passionate, rather raw as he dug into the notes, and totally Russian in feeling. Dushkin! He must be the answer to the riddle. Balanchine must have heard him on a recording too.

Of course this is conjecture, but there is no underestimating the influence a performer can exert on one's perception of music or dance. My first response to *Duo Concertant*, particularly the intimacy I felt between the dancers and musicians, hinged on the slight, subtle glances exchanged among Peter Martins, Kay Mazzo, Lamar Alsop (the violinist), and Gordon Boelzner (the pianist). The way Martins slightly bowed his head while

New York City Ballet. Peter Martins and Kay Mazzo. *Duo Concertant.* Choreography by George Balanchine © Kay Mazzo. Photo by © Costas.

listening, the way Mazzo tilted hers; the fugitive smiles that passed between Mazzo and Alsop were as much a fabric of the ballet as the choreography itself. It all felt spontaneous, tender, incredibly alive. These details are fugitive, too. Today, *Duo Concertant* sometimes feels like a lesson in music appreciation. In better days today there are traces of the original spontaneity, where all four artists live totally in the present moment, enjoying the music and each other.

Ballo della Regina

1978

Premiered toward the end of Balanchine's career, *Ballo della Regina* takes technique to a level of sophistication that is unsurpassed. Although there is a trace of story drawn from the Verdi opera to which it is set, *Don Carlos*, its subject is technique. *Ballo* celebrates technique at far ends of the spectrum. At one end, it is a platform for delicious virtuoso dancing, "virtuoso" being the description Balanchine himself applied to his intentions. Yet part of its virtuosity springs from one of the most rudimentary facets of classical technique.

Soon after ballet students begin their studies, they learn the codified positions of the body—*croisé*, *effacé*, and *écarté*, as well as front, side, and back. These positions are usually learned with arm and leg movements that fill out the picture the body makes. These positions place the dancer at different angles to the audience, thus animating the dancer's line in a seemingly infinite number of ways. A dancer can do the same step, yet it will look totally different depending on which position he or she is in. The contrasts between the directly front, side, and back directions and the subtle positions in between are one reason why ballet is always lively to the eye. Each position carries its distinctive tonal and emotional coloration, and watching dancers move among them all is enlivening to one's mind and heart as well.

There is no ballet in which Balanchine does not capitalize on the visual delights of these different positions, but in *Ballo* he makes a big deal of it. Just about every movement the dancers do (especially the ballerina and the four women soloists) is at an angle to the audience. What makes the exercise rise to virtuoso level is the speed at which the dancing unfurls. The image of light passing through a prism is so often applied to fast dancing that it's a cliché. In *Ballo*, the image is the plain truth. Turning slightly this way and that, at a fast—damn fast—clip, the dancers sparkle. Even in the slow pas de deux, the ballerina throws off a sparkle or two. I'm thinking of her *grand développé* to the side, except that instead of facing front she's facing a back corner. I suppose it's the grandeur of the step done in the shade, as it were, that makes the moment so surprising. It makes one blink.

When students go through the basic positions, they are tracing a semi-circle; if they repeat the whole sequence on the opposite foot, they've come full circle. As they move, they're posing at about every twenty-fifth degree of the circle. That's a pretty precise demarcation, but in *Ballo* Balanchine

New York City Ballet. Ib Andersen and Merrill Ashley. *Ballo della Regina.* Choreography by George Balanchine © The George Balanchine Trust. Photo by © Costas.

sets out to mark off all three hundred and sixty degrees of the circle. He has the ballerina make very small hops on pointe in a circle (and on a straight leg, so as to make the rotation all the quicker), so that we see not only front, side, and back but all the points en route. We know what a second hand on a watch looks like; in *Ballo*, Balanchine proposes to show a dancer moving with the precision of a second hand. Like everything else in the ballet, the effect is amazing and delightful. You say to yourself, Now I know what a circle *really* looks like, from its inner stuffing on out.

Ballo also shows us what really fast footwork looks like. We see it right from the outset, when the ensemble of twelve ladies squeeze in a tiny *pas de bourrée*, or three-step maneuver, when a single shift from one foot to the other would suffice to catch the filigree of Verdi's music. Pushing filigree to its maximum is the name of the game. For the ensemble, the crest of the busy-busy-busy feet comes in the coda, when the ladies fly back and forth across the stage, yet still find time for those minuscule *pas de bourrée*. The ballerina's deftness reaches a peak when she circles the stage in chattering, giggling runs. Sometimes the audience giggles along with her feet, so infectious is the folderol.

Of course, Balanchine would not have been able to concoct these challenges without a dancer able to bring them to fruition. In 1978 he had Merrill Ashley, a specialist in allegro dancing. Ashley had the gift of clarity. No matter how fast and complex the choreography, Ashley showed it to us in black and white, with no blur around the edges. She had an absolute sense of space; she made clear the distinction between front and really front. So with Ashley as an accomplice, Balanchine could play with the questions, Why move from A to B in a straight line when you can get there in zigs and zags? Why do two steps on one count if three is more fun? Ashley herself collaborated with Balanchine in the game. In her book *Dancing for Balanchine* she describes the creation of *Ballo* and how she made life a trifle more difficult for herself in the final moments of the ballet. The ballerina lifts her leg high in *développé à la seconde* and then brings it down into *passé*—not in one fell swoop but in four notches, which she compares to stop-action images. Ashley then figured out on her own that in order to make the images sharper, she had to make a tiny upward movement of her leg before it lowered into the next notch. The dancer adds her bit of icing to Balanchine's, and you're in calorie heaven.

New York City Ballet. Merrill Ashley. *Ballo della Regina*. Choreography by George Balanchine © The George Balanchine Trust. Photo by © Costas.

Actually, *Ballo* takes place underwater, in a grotto inhabited by a fisherman who is searching for the perfect pearl, which he will present to the Queen of Spain. This is Verdi's setting for "La Peregrina," the divertissement music from *Don Carlos*. In acknowledgment of Verdi's libretto for the divertissement, the costumes for *Ballo* have a sheen reminiscent of mother-of-pearl. At one point the cavalier circles the stage as though he is searching for something or someone—the perfect pearl?—and in her first, brief duet with him the "pearl" makes swimming motions with her arms. But the arm motions that truly capture the spirit of the ballet occur at the very beginning, when each dancer in the ensemble spins one wrist around the other as her arms move forward. The spinning motion alludes to the stock nineteenth-century mime that says, "Let's dance." Yes, let's dance. That's *Ballo*.

It was a late bloomer. A small, compact ballet, it was somewhat eclipsed by *Vienna Waltzes*, a long and lavish ballet that was the highlight of the preceding spring season in 1977. I, for one, took to *Ballo* right off the bat, but it was generally regarded as yet another of Balanchine's openers, delightful but small potatoes. It has grown in stature over the years, and that makes sense. With its eye on technical connoisseurship, it speaks to the heart of Balanchine's art. And in its embodiment of joy, it speaks to the heart of all dance.

Suggested Reading

Ashley, Merrill. *Dancing for Balanchine.* New York: E. P. Dutton, 1985.

Buckle, Richard, and John Taras. *George Balanchine: Ballet Master.* New York: Random House, 1988.

Choreography by George Balanchine: A Catalogue of Works. New York: Viking Penguin, 1984.

Costas. *Balanchine: Celebrating a Life in Dance.* Windsor, Conn.: Tide-Mark Press, 2003.

Farrell, Suzanne. *Holding On to the Air.* Gainesville: University Press of Florida, 2002.

Fisher, Barbara Milberg. *In Balanchine's Company.* Middletown, Conn.: Wesleyan University Press, 2006.

Garis, Robert. *Following Balanchine.* New Haven, Conn.: Yale University Press, 1995.

Goldner, Nancy. *The Stravinsky Festival of the New York City Ballet.* New York: Eakins Press, 1973.

Gottlieb, Robert. *George Balanchine: The Ballet Maker.* New York: HarperCollins Publishers, 2004.

Gottschild, Brenda Dixon. *Digging the Africanist Presence in American Performance.* Westport, Conn.: Praeger, 1996.

Joseph, Charles M. *Stravinsky & Balanchine: A Journey of Invention.* New Haven, Conn.: Yale University Press, 2002.

Kent, Allegra. *Once a Dancer . . .* New York: St. Martin's Press, 1997.

Kirstein, Lincoln. *Thirty Years of the New York City Ballet.* New York: Alfred A. Knopf, 1978.

Maiorano, Robert, and Valerie Brooks. *Balanchine's Mozartiana.* New York: Freundlich Books, 1985.

Martins, Peter. *Far From Denmark.* Boston: Little, Brown and Company, 1982.

Mason, Francis. *I Remember Balanchine.* New York: Doubleday, 1991.

131

Reynolds, Nancy. *Repertory in Review*. New York: Dial Press, 1977.

Schorer, Suki, and Russell Lee. *Suki Schorer on Balanchine Technique*. Gainesville: University Press of Florida, 2006.

Tallchief, Maria. *America's Prima Ballerina*. Gainesville: University Press of Florida, 2005.

Taper, Bernard. *Balanchine: A Biography*. New York: Times Books, 1984.

Villella, Edward. *Prodigal Son*. New York: Simon and Schuster, 1992.

Volkov, Solomon. *Balanchine's Tchaikovsky*. New York: Simon and Schuster, 1985.

Nancy Goldner has written about dance for *The Nation*, the *Christian Science Monitor*, the *Philadelphia Inquirer*, *Dance Now* (London), and other publications. She is the author of *The Stravinsky Festival of the New York City Ballet* (1973) and a member of the editorial board of the *International Encyclopedia of Dance*.